THE CHALLENGE OF EXCELLENCE, VOL I.

LEARNING THE ROPES OF CHANGE

Scout Lee, Ed.D.
Jan Summers, Ed.D.

Portland, Oregon

Published by

METAMORPHOUS PRESS

P.O. Box 10616
Portland, Oregon 97210

Copyright © 1990, 1984 by Excellence Unlimited, Inc.

All rights reserved. No material in this book may be copied, reproduced, or used in any way without written permission from the author.

Lee, Scout, 1944 —
  The challenge of excellence / Scout Lee.
   p.   cm.
  Contents: v. 1. Learning the ropes of change.
  ISBN 1-55552-004-9 (v. 1) : $16.95
   1. Mind and body. 2. Success. 3. Neurolinguistic programming. 4. Outward bound schools. I. Title.
BF161.L44   1989
158 -- dc20   89-12955
                                                             CIP

Typesetting by Cy–Ann Designs, Portland, Oregon
Printed in U.S.A.

DEDICATION

Always it is you, Blue, who insists that I constantly accept "The Challenge of Excellence." Without your strong support, my gift would be less courageously and joyfully given. So, this is dedicated to you, Blue, my playmate for all seasons.

Special "Thank You"

My twin sister, Dr. Jan summers, has always been my dreaming partner. She knows me well and has the ability to take my ideas and "grow" them. Thank you, Sister, for believing in my vision and for helping me dance it awake.

And to you extraterrestrial beings that teach me when I have the softness to allow you in . . . keep the information flowing.

iv

Table of Contents

DEDICATION iii
FOREWORD vii
PART I 1
   1 PRINCIPLES 3
   2 COLLAPSED REALITIES OR INTEGRATION   11
   3 TECHNIQUES FOR "PAYING ATTENTION" . 17
   4 FULL BODY CALIBRATION 29
   5 TRACKING 35
   6 THE PLAY FRAME 43
   7 TAKING IT HOME 53
PART II 57
   8 WELCOME TO THE CHALLENGE OF
      EXCELLENCE 59
   9 INITIATION TO LEARNING THE ROPES . . 63
   10 THE LOW ELEMENTS 73
   11 PATTERNS OF THE MIND
      MIRRORED BY THE BODY 81
   12 THE LOW ELEMENTS 107
   13 CALIBRATING A GROUP 121
   14 CHALLENGE ELEMENTS FOR GROUPS . 127

15 PATTERNS OF BEHAVIOR ON
   GROUP CHALLENGES 133
16 UTILIZATION OF GROUP INTERACTION
   PATTERNS 139
17 THE HIGH ELEMENTS 141
18 CONCLUSION AND NEW BEGINNINGS . 165

FOREWORD

The Challenge of Excellence, Vol I is about utilizing "challenge" and "playfulness" to program the human computer for "excellence." Our life "experience" *is* our "program." It is our "experience" of life that "programs" the nervous system, or creates the habits and patterns from which we act. What we actually *DO* provides the library of human software from which we can select programs of action. At any moment in time 90% of what is fed into the brain is proprioceptive, i.e., movement in space. *Movement is the broadest pathway for programming the human brain. What better way to program "success" than to create movement patterns necessary to succeed!*

To call a human being a "human computer" is a compliment and a reality. We are the finest of computers. Our bodies are the metaphor from which sprang all the wonders of computer technology. We created pumps and engines out of our experience of having a heart. We created computers out of our experience of having a brain.

"Excellence" simply means to *utilize energy to the maximum efficiency. All energy! It is a choice to have maximum abundance* in our lives with ease. To "effort" is to waste energy.

The idea of utilizing "challenge" experiences to elicit and install patterns of excellence came to us in 1980. It seemed to us to be a return of something old and powerful, for surely our ancestors challenged themselves by climbing, swinging, and balancing as a means of basic survival. Our experience with challenge ropes courses seemed to maximize challenge in the most streamlined way. Though we use many forms of "challenge," we find the concept of ropes courses to be the most elegant in terms of utilizing the *most* movement patterns in the *shortest* amount of time with the *largest* number of people. This made it possible for us to bring high quality training to groups of players who would otherwise not have access.

Who knows where the idea of ropes courses first came from? What human being built the first bridge or swing? We understand that George Hebert of the French army was the first to use ropes courses to train groups of soldiers, and Father Raoul Cloutier and George Gauvream brought the idea to the North American continent. Project Adventure and Outward Bound dared to use ropes courses for physical education and thus paved the way for their even more elegant use today.

While ropes courses were establishing themselves in the mainstream, other powerful new technologies to access or understand the human computer (the mind/body) were being developed. NeuroLinguistic Programming (NLP) and Feldenkrais were among the finest, and provided us tools to better utilize movement and communication as a pathway for "choice" in an age of rapid transformation. The Excellence Principle utilized in *The Challenge of Excellence* is a tapestry woven of our love for the ropes and our deep understanding of these advanced communication and movement principles.

We share simply, totally from our own experience . . . our own model. Our gift is intended to spread the good news . . . "achieving excellence can be both fun and challenging." Please accept our personal "Challenge of Excellence."

Scout Lee
Jan Summers

PART I

2 CHALLENGE OF EXCELLENCE

1

PRINCIPLES

Principles are gateways one must walk through in order to truly experience **self worth** and have the courage to give that understanding freely. In the spirit of the legendary "Tinkerbell" we "believe" the following:

- Each one of us must learn to experience our self worth continually.
- We must face ourselves and step inside what we see.
- We must never give up.
- The more we **wish for**, the more wonderful life is.
- We each **create** our own reality.
- To really live is to take responsibility for our own creation.
- Playfulness is the behavior of enlightenment.
- Let's begin by talking about the principles behind these basic beliefs and how they relate to **excellence**.

4 CHALLENGE OF EXCELLENCE

1. **THE BODY IS THE MESSENGER OF THE MIND**. The first and most basic concept to be understood is that no movement can be executed unless it has been encoded or programmed in the nervous system. Likewise, the movement patterns that are encoded in the nervous system determine the behavioral capabilities of the human animal. A manager, for example, cannot divide harmony and balance from dispute unless his or her own body understands and can execute **balance**. The mind generates thoughts based on the actual **experience** of the body. Likewise, the body *is* the experience of the mind. We have been given a body that we might feel our thoughts, and a mind that we might understand the message of our body. The cycle is unending. By understanding and observing the body and its movement through space we can understand the operation of the mind. Placed in a spontaneous situation, the body can only execute the patterns of programs encoded or already punched into the nervous system.

Challenge ropes courses more than any other single activity allow us the opportunity to observe the patterns coded in the nervous system. Patterns of **balance**, setting an **outcome**, **initiating** a task, **executing** a task, **completing** a task, executing a **recovery** strategy, **coaching** or **criticizing** oneself, **overcoming** an obstacle, **walking** a line, **building** a team, **motivating** a team, **reaching** the top, **leaping** into the unknown, **developing** a partnership, **rising** from a fall, **straddling** the line, **extending** oneself, **trusting**, and many more patterns are immediately observable on the Challenge of Excellence Ropes Course.

In order to offer a person choices about successful patterns of functioning it is first necessary to know the patterns they currently use. New possibilities of behavior must then be actually installed through **movement** in order to program the nervous system to execute that pattern automatically. **Experience**, not reason, is necessary

Principles 5

for habits of success to be formed. Learning to calibrate or track (stalk) the movement of a body through space is analogous to reading a computer printout of the mind.

Because the mind/body is one and we seek to understand the mind, it makes sense to access the recesses of the mind through observing the partner of the human experience that is observable . . . **the body**! With the technology presented in this book, understanding and programming the human computer for success is taken out of the realm of the mysterious and made available to any who would learn. To use movement and challenge to program the human computer for success is far more satisfying and effective than the typical academic drills executed by business and therapy today. It is also eons more inviting and fun!

Last summer we enlarged our business. The move involved risk, both personal and financial. We wanted to be able to get on a roll and "go for it" with no "stalls" or "hesitations." No amount of coaching, pep talks, or counseling could have done for us what the river did. Brooke, Chris, and I scheduled a six day river trip with friends. Our sole intention was to utilize the trip to insure that our bodies could keep a roll going through any obstacles . . . and to pace ourselves.

We snuck out of camp at midnight and took off for the Green River in Utah.

The river proved to be a powerful metaphor for life. At times it was calm and flowed easily along. We floated in our tubes or swam along side the rafts. At other times we battened down for storms or lazily basked in the sun along the canyon floor. Sometimes we fought for our very lives as we rowed wildly through eight foot standing walls of waves rolling back on themselves. It was at these times particularly that we learned to "keep a roll going."

"Rattlesnake Canyon's one mile ahead!" The signal sent us into high activity. It was rated a seven on the scale

6 CHALLENGE OF EXCELLENCE

and had high standing waves and treacherous rock walls. The river, unlike a ride at the fair, doesn't stop! It just keeps rollin' along. The signal brought us out of our tubes and into the rafts. On went our tennis shoes and life–jackets. We knew we had to hit the eight foot wall fast and dead center. To do otherwise was to risk being trapped in its suck hole at the bottom. The idea of going overboard with no life jacket and **walking out** of the suck hole on the bottom of the river was not an appealing thought. It simply meant **"seeing the wall," "buckling up for it," "hanging on,"** and **"rowing precisely and fast."** There was no time for hesitation!

Over and over again we crashed through standing waves and rapids. Over and over again we connected this **pattern** being coded in our nervous systems to **"roll on the river of life."** Our minds could now conceive of risk differently when away from **"challenge,"** we learned to PREPARE for it and pay FULL ATTENTION through it. Not only did we have a wonderful six day vacation, but we also programmed our computers to quadruple our business! The Challenge of Excellence Ropes course allows us to do the same thing for far more people in a shorter period of time. The Challenge of Excellence is a computer programming course. YOU are the computer. The program is "EXCELLENCE" . . . YOUR EXCELLENCE!

2. **FIND WHAT WORKS AND GROW IT**. This is our second basic principle. It is more useful to discover **what works** for a person and **grow it** than to focus on what doesn't work. If a person has **weaknesses** the only way they'll gain new choices is by utilizing whatever **strengths** they have. A "mistake" is a statement about a direction taken. To focus on the "mistake" directs the person away from their original intention. To draw attention to the "mistake" negates the embarked upon outcome. "Problem Solving Models" are a **"problem"**! They spend enor-

mous amounts of time deciphering the **"problem"** rather than re–directing energy toward the desired result or outcome. Institutions have been built to study mistakes, leaving behind any remembrance of what was desired to begin with. To study a mistake rather than maintaining a focus on the outcome is like a sailor resetting a compass with each change of wind direction. If the **"intention"** is to sail north, the sailor sets his compass or intention to sail north. If the winds are out of the north, the sailor must tack to the northeast and then the northwest. It is still his intention to arrive in the north. It would be wasting energy to constantly re–direct his compass with each changing wind. To focus on a problem, creates it! To focus on an outcome brings it within our grasp and programs our computer for success.

3. **WE GET WHAT WE PAY ATTENTION TO**. During war times torpedoes were programmed to track submarines. The tracking device in the submarine was called a servo–mechanism. It had one outcome: find and destroy the submarine. When the torpedo got off track, the servo–mechanism activated to bring the torpedo back on track. Its attention was always on the submarine. The servo–mechanism for the human computer is our **focus of attention**. What we **see** in our mind's eye, face or don't face with our bodies, and/or talk about silently or otherwise is precisely what we get. It's a law of basic physics. The way we utilize energy is the exact energy pattern we bring to ourselves. It can be no other way. We literally create our own experience. If we **waste** things, we bring **waste** or **garbage** into our lives.

All there is, is energy . . . quantums . . . building blocks of life. All that is, is energy . . . dancing a particular dance at a particular rate of speed which creates the illusion of form or formlessness. The smaller the space that the energy moves in, the faster the velocity of movement

8 CHALLENGE OF EXCELLENCE

and the greater the density of the form. When we think a thought, (i.e. see a picture in our mind's eye, or say a word, or feel a vibration), we vibrate quantums or units of energy equivalent to that thought. Those quantums are both **magnetic** and **reflective**. The vibration of quantums created by the act of **"thinking"** summons other quantums vibrating the same dance. In the world of quantum physics, to think a thought is to send out an announcement in the universe for all quantums vibrating that dance (thought or word) to come running to join together. To think a thought repeatedly is to gather enough quantums or energy building blocks to create the physical manifestation of the thought. Energy is magnetic. It loves to join a family unit. It loves to dance together and seeks its own vibration. A thought is a powerful form of moving energy. Consider the fact that in the breath you just took, you breathed in 10 trillion units of energy! Imagine how much more energy you move by speaking or walking or even nodding your head. To think a thought repeatedly brings the manifestation of that thought into your experience. This fact is doubly insured by energy's other property of **reflection**. Whatever thought we think or action we perform comes back to us. It must! It's the pattern of the energy we swirl around us. It's a literal statement, "We get exactly what we deserve," and "we deserve exactly what we have," be it grand or otherwise. *We are the creators of our own experience!* When we really **get this principle** we are free to use our human experience to create abundance and joy. This is our single intention . . . to make abundance and joy available through excellent utilization of energy. When we understand that we **create our own experience,** we can take responsibility for our creation.

4. **AWARENESS IMPROVES FUNCTION.** Calling players' attention to what and how they are doing adds

another dimension to each thing we do with them. Awareness without judgement is a first and very powerful element of change, and of taking home and utilizing what is gained. Carole is crossing the Burma Bridge, easily and gracefully, even though she has never done this sort of thing before. Saying to her, "Notice how easily and gracefully you do this new task. Be aware of how well your body works for you, even without practice," gives her walk an extra dimension. On the same element, Cliff has his knees locked and his feet tight, gripping hard with his hands, but he is quite unconscious of this in his effort to do well. Saying, "Notice your feet and legs. Are they tight or relaxed? Notice your hands. Allow yourself to find ease on this bridge. Use only the effort needed," gives him the opportunity to try a more relaxed and workable way. Before you called his attention, his efforting and tension were unconscious and therefore not easy to change. Making him aware of what he was doing, suggesting a possible alternative, gives him awareness of some different way to approach this, and thus opens up choice. Given true choice, the player will always choose that which works best, freeing himself to be his best. **Awareness** is the beginning of this chain of events which leads to choice. It's not that Cliff shouldn't grip tight; that is a useful behavior . . . sometimes. What you want to offer without judgement are choices; then he can feel and choose which one works best for him in this situation, thereby improving his functioning.

Many people in our society have learned to numb themselves and be unaware. A small, active child goes into a classroom and is made to sit for seemingly endless hours. This may be very uncomfortable and aggravating, but over time, the child learns to ignore this bodily feedback or be punished. A man in a business meeting finds something very funny, yet it is inappropriate to laugh. He stops himself and stops his natural process. Time and

10 CHALLENGE OF EXCELLENCE

time again this happens, until many players will be very unaware of their bodies or how they feel, what they like and want to do. Creating **awareness** of themselves, their feelings, and their bodies is a wonderful and very renewing gift. Creating awareness and attention as they perform their best allows them the conscious choice to recall these states and use them at will. Given awareness and choice, each person chooses excellence!

2

COLLAPSED REALITIES OR INTEGRATION

The propensity of the nervous system is to form habits or patterns. The same is true in physics. It is easy for energy to continue a movement that has become habituated or repeated. The process of change is the process of shifting out of a pattern or habit that doesn't work to one that works effectively and effortlessly. Talking about a habit or wishing for a change doesn't bring the change. TRYING to stop a pattern doesn't change it. The issue becomes one of find a way to **interrupt** a pattern of efforting needlessly in order to install new choices of moving with grace and ease. Our challenge is to **enlarge** the repertoire of patterns a person has available to them rather than destroy old patterns.

Problems exist because a person perceives a lack of resources. They are focused on **the problem**. In the nervous system a problem exists when the pattern of movement or maneuver coded doesn't achieve our hopes and aspirations. In order for the mind to conceive of new possibilities, the body must experience new patterns.

Every internal state has a unique sequence it runs in

12 CHALLENGE OF EXCELLENCE

the nervous system in order to sustain the state (i.e. balance, anger, creativity, despair, etc.). The body easily forms habits of how to move or not to move within each specific state. For example, when we feel excited the body has a habit of opening up, standing up, yelling, clapping, etc. When we feel scared, the body has a habit of closing down, quieting itself, etc. If we can bring the body posture of **excitement** to a scared internal state, we, in essence, force the nervous system to *re–program* the meaning of **scared** to include an alert body, versus the body closed off from input. The metaphor is simple. If a person is throwing rocks at us (figuratively speaking) we would be less likely to be hit if we face them directly, with flexibility to move in whatever direction necessary to avoid the onslaught of rocks.

The strategic move for bringing a resourceful body posture and pattern to a problematic frame of mind is called a **collapsed reality**. The meaning is literal. We collapse the reality of **limited choice** into the reality of **full choice**. This forces the nervous system to revise a program. All change is nothing more than an **integration** of resources or a **collapsed reality**. (Figure 1)

Understanding the concept of integration or collapsed realities gives us the ability to bring numerous workable patterns to states of mind deemed problematic. Again, our focus is on what works! Find what works and bring it in contact with that which lacks resources.

Collapsed Realities, or Integration 13

FIGURE 1

14 CHALLENGE OF EXCELLENCE

Bob had climbed our 34 foot pamper pole and was standing perfectly balanced on an eleven inch square over four stories in the air. There was nothing to cling to for support . . . only the hope of catching the swinging trapeze suspended 8 1/2 feet in the air in front of him. While standing on this small aerial platform, Bob was perfectly balanced in his body. He had to be in order to be there! It was the perfect time to **collapse** a reality. Bob had mentioned how "out–of–balance" his work was in relationship with his "play." This, in turn, created imbalance in his relationship to his wife and two children. Thus, while standing tall, open, and balanced, we shouted out reminders of these "imbalances." In a totally new body posture, Bob had to consider bringing **balance** to his life. Never before had Bob mulled over his relationship with his wife in this balanced body posture. His nervous system went wild recording all the old thought patterns to this new posture. Once on the ground, he stood tall as he chuckled about his relationship and very soon conceived of brilliant new ideas for enhancing the quality of his life. Having the pattern of balanced **wired in his body** made it possible for him to **think** more creatively. This simple but elegant maneuver is the secret to change. We'll model it repeatedly throughout this book. Simply frame the problem in something much bigger than the problem and integrate them together. (Figures 2 and 3)

INTEGRATE "PROBLEM" INTO WHAT WORKS!

FIGURE 2

FRAME "PROBLEM STATE" WITH POWERFUL EXPERIENCE!

Figure 3

3

TECHNIQUES FOR "PAYING ATTENTION"

Several years ago a psychotherapist and a linguistic professor joined in a search for a structure to the magic of successful communication. They had noticed that there were those particular professional communicators who seemed to sense precisely **where to tap** in bringing about useful behavior changes. The result of their long years of investigation is a communication model they call "NeuroLinguistic Programming." [1][2] By understanding verbal patterns. sequences, and body cues, they have been able to simplify the process of understanding another's thought patterns. The implications of NeuroLinguistic Programming and other meta–communication models will have a profound effect on our ability to assist others in structuring quality lifestyles.

When a person communicates **thoughts, feelings, perceptions,** and **beliefs,** we now know that they are attempt-

---

1 Bandler, R. and Grinder, J. *The Structure of Magic.* Palo Alto, California: Science and Behavior Books, Inc., 1975.
2 Grinder, J. and Bandler, R. *The Structure of Magic II.* Palo Alto, California: Science and Behavior Books, Inc., 1975.

18 CHALLENGE OF EXCELLENCE

ing to express something about a picture, a sound, or an internal feeling they are consciously or unconsciously experiencing. By observing that "something about their bodies and the shift of their eyes" we can know which they are experiencing and in what sequence. Combined with the syntax of their language, we can closely approximate our lifelong desire to "be a little mouse in the corner of another's mind." Thought processes include the following strategies:

1. We can actually produce a film of how we believe something could be or appear in the future.
2. We can replay a movie we made in the past.
3. We can produce unique sounds, such as thinking of the way to phrase a question.
4. We can listen to tape recordings we have made in the past.
5. We can listen to or construct complete dialogues between two or more people.
6. We can experience the special effects of kinesthetic sensations of the pictures and tapes in our mind.

These **thinking** strategies might be simplified to resemble a three–story production studio in our minds. The top floor of our mind's studio has two rooms: one for producing new films and one for replaying the "oldies but goodies" of our past experience. The second floor enriches our production potential with full sound effects. One studio creates new sound and another replays cassette recordings made in the past. The bottom floor of the studio of our mind houses the special effects staff, capable of adding feelings and responses to our experience. A special room for audiotape dialogue is also housed here. In most cases it is not surprising to notice that the shift of a person's eyes (as well as numerous body parts) tells the observer precisely which studio the individual is in or avoiding. (Figure 4 shows the eye scanning patterns and Figure 5 enlarges the pattern to include the studios of the mind and their connection to the whole body.)

EYE ACCESSING MOVEMENTS FOR A "NORMALLY ORGANIZED" RIGHT-HANDED PERSON

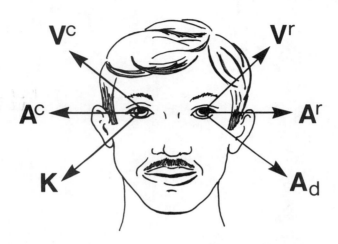

V^c = Visual Constructed or Reconstructed Images
(Eyes up and right)

*Eyes defocused or unmoving also indicate visual accessing. Calibrate the rest of body for recall or constructed images.

A^c = Auditory Constructed sounds or words
(Eyes horizontal and to the right)

K = Kinesthetic Feelings, including smell and taste.
(Eyes move down and right)

V^r = Visual Recall (Eidetic) Images
(Eyes up and left)

A^r = Auditory recall sounds or words. Tonality, etc. seems most important here.
(Eyes horizontal and to the left)

A_d = Auditory sounds or words. Words move to the forefront and conversation is present
(Eyes are down and left)

Techniques for "Paying Attention" 21

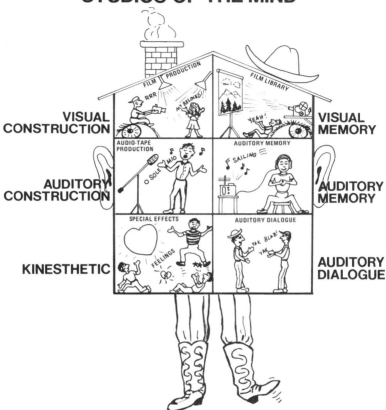

22 CHALLENGE OF EXCELLENCE

After years of exploration, John Grinder and Richard Bandler developed the NLP Model to assist us in organizing specific information (1979). Everyone has, at most, five sensory systems through which they contact physical reality. These senses, the eyes, ears, skin, nose, and tongue are the input systems or input channels. Sensory distinctions are made within these channels, especially within the kinesthetic, visual, and auditory channels (K, V, and A). using these three sensory systems, input can be observed, directed, shaped, *conditioned*, and even switched. Information *INPUT* in our systems is processed distinctly unique to each individual and is expressed as *OUTPUT* in the form of verbal and non-verbal language.

Verbal Output: Predicates. In NLP, verbal language is important to the extent that predicates used allow us to know what part of the internal representation of experience is most important to the person. Notice that the adjectives, adverbs, and verbs that people select to use reveal which sensory system they are most aware of at the moment:

Person: "I'm so <u>bored</u>. (Eyes look down to the right and left hand moves to the sternum). When I <u>lived</u> in the city, there was so much to <u>get into</u>. Here I just <u>sit</u> in front of the T.V."

Modeler: "Now let me <u>see</u> if I understand you. I'd like a <u>clear</u> <u>perspective</u> on your problem. Could you <u>focus</u> specifically on your problem so I can <u>see</u> a <u>picture</u> of how you're bored?

The person is only aware of the <u>kinesthetic</u> portion of experience, while the modeler is aware of the <u>visual</u> part of experience. This is a major source of miscommunication. (See Figure 6)

Techniques for "Paying Attention" 23

Non–Verbal Output: Internal Responses to External Behavior. Though people are only aware of portions of their experiences, information is being processed in all systems. Other non–verbal cues signal the trained communicator regarding the internal process or experience. Hand gestures, posture, head position, breathing rates, tempo of speech, tonality and pitch of speech, facial tonus changes, skin color changes, and body temperature are some of the more subtle clues to internal experience. The most obvious systems of Kinesthetic, Visual, and Auditory channels is the systematic shifting of the eyes to access and store information. Figure 7 interprets the meaning of our various eye shifts and indicates <u>how</u> a person is "thinking" or "chunking together" pieces of information.

This internal processing of information is called the 4–TUPLE (meaning 4 variable)d and is a systematic, primary internal experience utilizing the VISUAL, AUDITORY, KINESTHETIC, AND OLFACTORY CHANNELS. All experience is composed of these primary parts and is represented as follows:

PRIMARY EXPERIENCE

or $\quad\quad\quad\quad <V^{ie}, A^{ie}, O^{ie}>$

4–TUPLE

We can also show the 4–TUPLE as follows: (Dilts, Grinder, Bandler, Bandler, DeLozier, 1980).

24 CHALLENGE OF EXCELLENCE

MATCHING PREDICATES WITH ACCESSING CUES

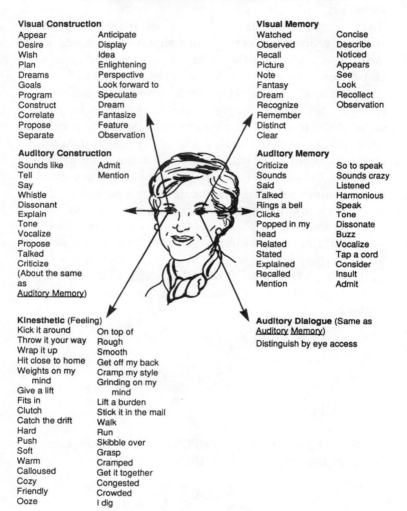

Visual Construction
Appear, Anticipate
Desire, Display
Wish, Idea
Plan, Enlightening
Dreams, Perspective
Goals, Look forward to
Program, Speculate
Construct, Dream
Correlate, Fantasize
Propose, Feature
Separate, Observation

Auditory Construction
Sounds like, Admit
Tell, Mention
Say
Whistle
Dissonant
Explain
Tone
Vocalize
Propose
Talked
Criticize
(About the same as Auditory Memory)

Visual Memory
Watched, Concise
Observed, Describe
Recall, Noticed
Picture, Appears
Note, See
Fantasy, Look
Dream, Recollect
Recognize, Observation
Remember
Distinct
Clear

Auditory Memory
Criticize, So to speak
Sounds, Sounds crazy
Said, Listened
Talked, Harmonious
Rings a bell, Speak
Clicks, Tone
Popped in my head, Dissonate
Related, Buzz
Stated, Vocalize
Explained, Tap a cord
Recalled, Consider
Mention, Insult
Admit

Kinesthetic (Feeling)
Kick it around, On top of
Throw it your way, Rough
Wrap it up, Smooth
Hit close to home, Get off my back
Weights on my mind, Cramp my style
Give a lift, Grinding on my mind
Fits in, Lift a burden
Clutch, Stick it in the mail
Catch the drift, Walk
Hard, Run
Push, Skibble over
Soft, Grasp
Warm, Cramped
Calloused, Get it together
Cozy, Congested
Friendly, Crowded
Ooze, I dig

Auditory Dialogue (Same as Auditory Memory)
Distinguish by eye access

FIGURE 6

Techniques for "Paying Attention" 25

SUBTLE ACCESSING CUES

Other sets of accessing cues require more subtle observation than eye-scanning patterns. These are briefly described in tabular form:

ACCESS CUE	REPRESENTATIONAL SYSTEM INDICATED			
	VISUAL	AUDITORY	KINESTHETIC	OTHER SPECIFIED
1. Breathing	top of chest/ rapid, jerky/ shallow	solar plexus smooth/even inhale and exhale	abdomen/ slow/deep	
2. Facial skin and muscle tone, skin color and texture	raised brows/ cheeks pulled upward/tight skin/ less color in cheeks or spotty	cheeks pulled toward ears	jowls sagging/ cheeks relaxed/ color even in cheeks/even flush on face	
3. Moisture level on skin	increasing ➡ ➡ ➡ ➡ ➡			
4. Pupil size	smoothly varying	little variation/ slow variation	may show extreme dilation or constriction in rapid but infrequent size changes	
5. Pulse	rapid/shallow	very even rhythm/ medium rate	slow/deep/even/ pulse may be highly visible	
6. Body postures, gestures	upward head tilt/ hand gestures upward shoulders up back and forth steps	telephone postures with cocked head hand to ear/ hand gestures to side of left weighing of body	hand movements to lower body, midline movement in left hand, foot	(gustatory) swallowing, lip and tongue movements weighing on right leg-movement in right foot, hand (olfactory) flared nostrils
7. Voice	higher pitch/ varying rate/ varying pitch	even rhythm/ even pitch/ tone continuous	lower pitch/ slow/ slowly varying pitch and rate	

FIGURE 7

26 CHALLENGE OF EXCELLENCE

Movement through these systems may be mapped by following the cues previously mentioned, such as eye scanning patterns, breathing rates, changes in posture, pitch of voice, tempo of speech, etc. As information is processed internally, changes in breathing, muscle tone, skin color, lip size, etc. also results. These resulting external changes are known as BMIR'S (Behavioral Manifestations of Internal responses). By systematically associating these BMIR'S to external stimuli, the MODELER is able to "Calibrate" (match external cues to internal experience and resulting BMIR'S) the structure of a person's experience. The result is that the Modeler understands the <u>STRUCTURE</u> of behavior. Once we understand the structure of <u>experience</u>, we can change <u>HOW</u> a person **problemates** by making intentional changes in some component of the structure of experience. By re–organizing, adding to, deleting, or otherwise changing any component of the 4–TUPLE <V, A, K, O> of experience, we change the total experience.

The following are actual examples of the structure of defective verbal patterns. They program failure.

1. "When I'm presented with a challenge, my first response is to <u>tell myself</u> I don't understand and <u>can't</u> do it. I see myself crying in frustration. I tell myself that I never do anything that I'm totally happy with."

$$A^r \longrightarrow A^{c-} \longrightarrow V^{c-} \longrightarrow A^{r-} = K-$$

2. "When I'm asked to do something new and different, I <u>imagine failing</u> and begin to find ways to excuse myself. I usually end up feeling obligated to try and feel pressured."

$$A^r \longrightarrow V^{c-} \longrightarrow A^{c-} \;=\; K-$$

3. "I usually feel excited about trying new things. I imagine how fun it will be, but things <u>never seem</u> as fun as I told myself they would be."

$$V^{c+} \longrightarrow K+ \longrightarrow V^{m-} \longrightarrow A^c \;=\; K-$$

The most streamlined way we know to bring choices to a person's behavior is to change the kinesthetic portion of their experience. since the body is a very literal statement of the thought process it makes sense to shape that portion of the experience that is visible and not susceptible to distortion. We call this artistic maneuver "analog sculpting." We literally "sculpt" the human experience toward excellence by shaping the patterns of the body and attaching them to key words of the mind. Our constant challenge is "Change K." Reshape your body's pattern and your mind will follow. (Figure 8)

28 CHALLENGE OF EXCELLENCE

FIGURE 8

4

FULL BODY CALIBRATION

Full body calibration extends the use of eye scanning patterns and analog cues to the full body.

The analog or computer printout of the human body is far more elegant than we first imagined! Over the past two and a half years we've analyzed "miles" of video tape on hundreds of campers who journey to Oklahoma to accept "The Challenge of Excellence." For seven days they are fully immersed in acts and antics requiring their finest strategies for creating, solving problems, deciding, learning, motivating, and convincing others. We record the entire week and provide instant video feedback with "Full Body Calibration." (Figure 9)

30 CHALLENGE OF EXCELLENCE

FULL BODY CALIBRATION

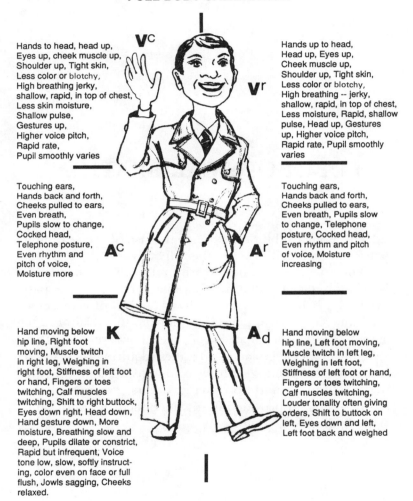

V^c
Hands to head, head up,
Eyes up, cheek muscle up,
Shoulder up, Tight skin,
Less color or blotchy,
High breathing jerky,
shallow, rapid, in top of chest,
Less skin moisture,
Shallow pulse,
Gestures up,
Higher voice pitch,
Rapid rate,
Pupil smoothly varies

V^r
Hands up to head,
Head up, Eyes up,
Cheek muscle up,
Shoulder up, Tight skin,
Less color or blotchy,
High breathing -- jerky,
shallow, rapid, in top of chest,
Less moisture, Rapid, shallow
pulse, Head up, Gestures
up, Higher voice pitch,
Rapid rate, Pupil smoothly
varies

A^c
Touching ears,
Hands back and forth,
Cheeks pulled to ears,
Even breath,
Pupils slow to change,
Cocked head,
Telephone posture,
Even rhythm and
pitch of voice,
Moisture more

A^r
Touching ears,
Hands back and forth,
Cheeks pulled to ears,
Even breath, Pupils slow
to change, Telephone
posture, Cocked head,
Even rhythm and pitch
of voice, Moisture
increasing

K
Hand moving below
hip line, Right foot
moving, Muscle twitch
in right leg, Weighing in
right foot, Stiffness of left foot
or hand, Fingers or toes
twitching, Calf muscles
twitching, Shift to right buttock,
Eyes down right, Head down,
Hand gesture down, More
moisture, Breathing slow and
deep, Pupils dilate or constrict,
Rapid but infrequent; Voice
tone low, slow, softly instruct-
ing, color even on face or full
flush, Jowls sagging, Cheeks
relaxed.

A_d
Hand moving below
hip line, Left foot moving,
Muscle twitch in left leg,
Weighing in left foot,
Stiffness of left foot or hand,
Fingers or toes twitching,
Calf muscles twitching,
Louder tonality often giving
orders, Shift to buttock on
left, Eyes down and left,
Left foot back and weighed

Full Body Calibration   31

We've repeatedly noticed the following using Full Body Calibration.

1. "Integrated" states are easily calibrated by the following:
   — The heart region is open and aligned directly over or in front of the buttocks.
   — The eyes are soft, moist, and blinking.
   — Breathing is full and constant, an even flow.
   — Eye accessing cues are extremely diminished. Often no shifts are noticed.
   — Body is balanced and symmetrical.

2. People access differently when in "disassociated" states. Information both elicited and retrieved from "integrated" states is far more valuable.

3. "Disassociated" states (the state in which most folks live!) are detected by the following:
   — The heart region is "off balance," i.e., leaning back behind the buttocks or to one side or the other.
   — Eyes are hard, strained, sometimes dry, and unblinking.
   — Breathing stops, is often shallow, and is irregular.
   — Eye scanning patterns increase.

4. When people are standing and are weighed on the left foot, they are making an auditory lead or access (A^r or A_d).

5. Movement or tension in any part of the left leg or foot is indicative of an auditory access (A^r or A_d). the "rhythm" of the internal sounds is marked out by the movement or speed of movement.

6. When the left foot is pulled back and tense, you guess that the A^r or A_d is on "pause" and is "disassociated" (A^{rd} or A^d).

7. Tension or movement in the left hand lying in the lap, crossed behind the back, or hanging by the side marks out the nature of internal sounds in the auditory system

32 CHALLENGE OF EXCELLENCE

(A^r, A^d, or A^c), i.e. rhythm, disassociation.

8. Guess that the position of the hands is literal and ask about them, i.e., the index finger is pointing and the thumb is up = who are you shooting?"

— The left hand is holding the right hand down = A^l_d is holding on to feelings (K). "Ahhh, come on! You can 'let go' of your feelings!"

— The same is true for "squeezing," "patting," etc.

— Pressure on the toes or fingers of the left foot or hand computes as A^l_d (auditory internal dialogue). The cassette tapes of the mind are rolling. Ask the person to "turn up the volume so you can hear, too!"

10. Weight on the right leg while standing is a kinesthetic access (K).

11. Movement or tension in the right leg or foot gives literal information about kinesthetic access (feelings). Check out the movement, e.g., "shaking" — "feeling a little 'shaky' today?"

— Right foot propped up and pushing down or away

— Disassociated feelings (K^{id})

— "Go ahead, 'push' that feeling further away!"

— Right foot pulled up and held still at the ankle = feelings are on "hold."

12. The speed of the movement in the kinesthetic system is marked out by the rhythm of the observed movement in the right lower quadrant of the body.

13. Movement or tension when the right hand is in the lap, crossed behind the back, or hanging by the side signals variations of kinesthetic responses. Take the movement literally, i.e. right hand holding the left hand = feelings are quieting the internal voice.

14. Tight buttocks signals that the person is "holding feelings in."

15. Locked knees or elbows signal feelings that are "locked up." You can usually question this person's "flexibility" and get a powerful response.

Full Body Calibration 33

16. When the left leg is crossed over the right leg, the person is, in some way, "telling" self to "control" the feelings ($A^i_d = > K^{id}$).

17. When the arms are crossed over the chest with the hands tucked under, observe the movement of the fingers and hands. Movement in the left hand is A^r or A_d. Both of these accesses signal that the person is listening to recordings of the past. Movement in the right hand in this position signals A^c (auditory construction). When this access is preceded by a kinesthetic lead, the tonal quality of the voice heard is "most assuring" and is the "voice of the unconscious mind." Among the 300,000 tonal recordings of our auditory system, only one is the voice of our own unconscious ally. Some native American people call this the "familiar voice" or the "true voice," of the "spirit voice." Contact with this voice is indicative of the deepest level of rapport. Sequentially, this access will follow a kinesthetic access and looks like this ($K = > A^{iec}_F$). Translated, this is the auditory internal or external constructed familiar voice. When this voice (the Familiar voice) is heard, the body impulsively moves to action. This voice serves to positively instruct or coach. "Negatives" will not be heard.

18. When the right eyebrow is up, the person is visually constructing (V^c). When the left eyebrow is up, the person is visually remembering (V^l). The same is true for the lateral muscular twitches or movements of the face.

19. When the chest is caved in, the feelings are trapped and, thus, disassociated.

20. Mouth twitching or pulled back toward the ear(s) = internal talking, either A^i_d or A^c, depending on the side of the face the movement occurs.

21. Tension in the neck or throat — unexpressed A^i_d or A^c.

22. When the neck extends out in front of the shoulders, the person usually visually disassociates or imagines, then talks to self about the hallucinations. They are disassociated

34 CHALLENGE OF EXCELLENCE

from what is visually happening around them and their internal dialogue.

23. When a person sits Indian style with the right leg over the left, "feelings" are exposed. When the left leg is over the right, their feelings are "guarded" and they are either recording or talking.

There's lots more. TRACKING extends further the model of Full Body Calibration to observe the body "moving" in an environment. As we discuss the use of each element we'll offer specific examples.

5

TRACKING

Full body calibration takes the patterns of the face and enlarges them to the circle of the whole body. Now comes the exciting part; TRACKING: observing the whole body move in patterns in the larger circle of experience . . . and observing the patterns in and among the multiple circles of experience.

All living things move and leave their mark; the four–legged, the winged, the crawling things, the wind, and the human animal. These marks made by the movement of the human animal are, just like any other animal, observable and extremely valuable as direct feedback about the internal experience a person has. A basic understanding of quantum physics is to observe the smallest pattern of movement (or unit of energy) is to observe the largest pattern. The reverse is also true. To observe the largest pattern is to also see the smallest. For example, one may be seen "disassociating" by the pressing away from an object by the feet or hands. They may also be seen disassociating by sitting or moving on the periphery of a group,

36 CHALLENGE OF EXCELLENCE

or by reversing directions on a gaming field when the outcome is to move forward as quickly as possible. We have observed repeatedly that the person who **disassociates** does so as consistently with the chin as they do with their whole body pattern on a swinging log, across a conference table, or on a two mile gaming field of Indian Coup.

The body is the mind's experience of itself. How a person's body moves through space is how their mind processes information. Observing eye scanning patterns and minimal body cues gives information about HOW a person is thinking. Observing full–body movement through space gives information about HOW a person is thinking as well as WHAT they are thinking. The body and its selection of where to be in space is a literal metaphor of the human experience at the deepest of unconscious levels. When a body's pattern is repeated over and over again it will CREATE itself. Our bodies literally **act out** our thoughts. To **act out** a thought over and over again is to create the entire set of circumstances to sustain the drama. To see the larger patterns of a person's movements is to know their soul and to be able to predict with accuracy a person's future. TO INTERRUPT A PERSON'S PATTERNS IS TO CHANGE THE COURSE OF ONE'S DESTINY.

We now have the technology to OBSERVE patterns, to INTERRUPT patterns, to ELICIT patterns, to CREATE patterns, to INSTALL patterns, to MIMIC patterns, and to MODEL patterns. NLP and Feldenkrais have advanced our ability to reach our highest potential by allowing us the technology to SCAN FOR PATTERNS OF EXCEL-LENCE.

The more experiences we utilize to calibrate people the CLEARER our perspective is of their patterns of excellence and the more opportunity we have to mold their destiny toward their soul's intention.

For example, it is important that we all learn to "roll with the punches." This is a time of extremely rapid change,

Tracking 37

and "rolling with the punches" has definite survival value. Thus, have a person literally forward "roll" as they did when they were small. Both they and you will probably be surprised to find just how stiff and inflexible they have become. Stiffness and inflexibility of the body equals stiffness and inflexibility of the mind. To test this principle, calibrate the decision–making strategy of a supple–spined person with that of the ole' stiff–backed person. The person who can't do a graceful forward roll will calibrate a complex and lengthy decision–making strategy with a guaranteed visual or auditory access (disassociated) prior to any consideration of accessing kinesthetically. The person with the supple spine will run a very clean and integrated KAV loop. (That is, they'll feel their bodies, hear the sound of their own voices coaching, and see what is actually there to see.) **Teach a person how to do a fluid and graceful forward roll and you teach their mind to make fluid and graceful decisions.** Examples of tracking:

1. Joe is a stock broker. In his line of work there is one outcome: Make money for your clients. The moves necessary to achieve this outcome are far more complex than most businesses and are constantly shifting and changing. There is no time to despair over a wrong move made at nine a.m. because everything could be different twenty minutes later. It's essential that a stock broker stay alert and focused on the outcome. Quick recovery strategies are an absolute necessity for success. For Joe the **swinging log** became a great teacher of new choices for succeeding.

Suspended two feet off the ground and twenty–five feet in length, the swinging log models life when the **very foundation** of things are shaky. Shaky ground is an everyday experience in the stock market. Joe was, at first, unable to move at all. The log swings from side to side, back and forth, and twists. Quite a challenge! With assistance Joe moved a few steps and fell. Each fall brought an immedi-

38 CHALLENGE OF EXCELLENCE

ate reflex response of pain in his face and he cursed himself for his "clumsiness." ANY PATTERN REPEATED TWICE IS A HABIT. Two things were immediately obvious through tracking Joe's walk. First of all, Joe didn't know how to set and hold an outcome. Secondly, his recovery strategy wasted valuable time in focusing on the mistake rather than re–establishing the outcome. By holding his focus point on a mark on the tree directly at the end of the log he learned that his body adjusted to the moving log below him and he was able to **nail his eyes** on his outcome and keep moving.

He also discovered that by coaching himself **out loud** about his sensory experience he was able to realign his body each time he began to lose his balance, i.e., "There's a knot under my left foot. I'm moving slowly over it . . . breath, easy, Joe . . . Easy does it, Joe . . . I'm relaxing my shoulders, etc." We assured Joe that he could use the lessons of the swinging log by making the mark on the tree the outcome of making money, and the **coaching** a means of "rolling with the punches" in the stock market. TRACKING allowed us to offer this choice in a matter of moments, versus months or years.

2. A friend was heard to say of the mistakes in the studio she had just built, "Let the bloops remind you of my love in building it," as she was tripping over the cat lying in the middle of the floor. This is an example of a person who literally falls over backward to "please." Wouldn't it be much more pleasing to her loved one for her to walk upright, tall, poised, and graceful, focusing on the beauty of the gift? To give a person the experience of walking gracefully in the midst of reminders of those things that have caused them problems is to give that person the choice of **walking gracefully** through those problems. Where the full body is used to **collapse a resource** into a **problem state** the unconscious mind is more likely to repeat the

Tracking 39

pattern. The unconscious mind is the mind of a child and **the child** in us loves to MOVE! How much more elegant **change** would be if we would take walks to discuss new alternatives. The act of walking briskly and playfully while talking IS BRINGING AN ELEGANT AND SIMPLE CHOICE TO LIVING FULLY! Powerful and lasting change must be made in a FULL BODY PATTERN.

3. Peggy had never "walked a path alone." Even during the first five days of camp she was never seen alone. Her challenge to **walk** the path of Oklahoma rolling hills ALONE was metaphorically her first walk without the psychological crutches of support that had for fifty–six years kept her from taking the kinds of risks that would honor her spirit. After an hour and a half of walking alone, she found herself alone in the midst of an orchard. The blossoms were in full bloom and the air smelled of abundance and promised the same to her for her courage. Just at the moment that she realized both the ecstasy of her walk, and the agony of being ALONE, she was nudged from behind by a young horse named Oklahoma Sunshine Magic who had sneaked into the orchard and awaited the exact moment to remind Peggy that "she would not be alone if she takes a lone walk." Peggy was elated at the metaphoric promise of the horse and ran full–gaited back to the ranch to share her experience. Along the way she heard patting along the trail and turned to see Oklahoma Sunshine Magic following her home. She tearfully and gleefully shared her excitement at being followed. "Gosh, nobody's ever followed me." "Hell, girl, you ain't been goin' anywhere," was our teasing response.

Our skill as professional communicators is to be able to create the kinds of experiences for people that will allow them opportunity to model or move through their patterns. Patterns are much easier and more interesting to calibrate if they are large patterns that include multiple

40 CHALLENGE OF EXCELLENCE

variable of interaction. TRACKING enlarges the frame of calibration and yields rich resources for both experience and metaphor. How a person allows another to catch their body weight is how a person **trusts** support. How well two people can assist each other to the top of a forty foot dangle–duo is how they assist each other in life. How a group negotiates a sixteen foot wall is how they manage the **obstacles** of their professional or personal life. How a person leaps off a fifty foot platform into mid–air is precisely how they **step into the unknown**. How a person moves their "tribe" through two miles of unfamiliar territory under the cover of darkness is how they manage a team of people to focus on the same outcome. How people **dance** is a statement of their mutual fluidity. How people **walk** is a statement of how they can move from one point to another. How people play with each other is a statement of how well they're able to motivate others. Let us all dance and sing and tumble and walk and run with folks so that we can know them even more intimately! And in knowing them, offer them even more elegant patterns of movement so that they may have access to their own path of excellence in all things!

Tracking 41

TRACKING

42 CHALLENGE OF EXCELLENCE

6

THE PLAY FRAME

There have been rumors of late that a new Seer, called by some "The Seer of Playfulness", is now traveling the land. It was recently reported that this Seer was engaged in promoting a simple philosophy: WHEN YOU'RE PLAYING AND HAVING FUN, YOU'VE GOT ALL THE RESOURCES YOU'LL EVER NEED. Within the playfulness frame you're naturally kind, consistently fair, and personally powerful.

It is said that as this new Seer travels about, surprisingly little resistance is encountered. You may have already met the Seer if you've performed with elegance and excellence and enjoyed doing it. Even now, as you consider the possibility of again **playing** as a way of life, remember that whenever you have a question of procedure, no matter how small you consider it, simply pause and ask it of this Seer within you. Be assured that your answer will be in the next quiet thought!

You perhaps heard two answers and wondered which was the Seer's voice. Here is a simple test. One of your

44 CHALLENGE OF EXCELLENCE

thoughts included nudgings as to what you would enjoy doing now. That was the Seer's voice coming to you as your own thinking. The other thought, if there was one, suggested a reason for you to be anxious, but it offered no clear instructions. In one way or another, the Seer always says "Do THIS, for it will please you most, whereas the voice of playLESSness warns but never points clearly in any direction." *Adapted from Hugh Prather*

I'm an explorer — a "scout." The concept of the early Native American "scout" was "truthbearer" . . . the ears and eyes of the tribe, one who went out in front to detect danger or food and reported back to the people, the one who "cleared the way." In my personal adventure, I wear many hats: business woman, communication specialist, trainer, therapist, counselor, teacher, public speaker, rancher, scientist, researcher, spiritual leader, and healer. Central to all these roles is my unfaltering conviction that FUN, PLAYFULNESS, and HAPPINESS is in accordance with the HIGHEST of human excellence. When we value "playing" as a **way of life** we increase the value of living. I've seen thousands of case studies in my own research to validate the concept that **superior performances** come when folks are having FUN! I study HUMAN EXCELLENCE. Accessing, creating, and understanding "peak performances" is my great delight. And, after sixteen years of research, I'm convinced that PLAYFULNESS is not only the *mood* of excellence, but is the BASIC NATURE OF UNCONSCIOUSNESS OR THE DREAMER. The dreamer is PLAYFUL, ORNERY, AND FUN LOVING . . . ILLNESS AND DISHARMONY IS ONLY THE DREAMER POUTING BECAUSE IT ISN'T HAVING FUN! It's the "dreamer's" way of trying to get us to LIVE FULLY OUR DREAMS.

From the beginning of civilization, philosophers have been repeating that play is the supreme manifestation of human freedom. Plato argued that life must be lived as "play." Fredrich Schiller felt that man is completely a man only when he plays, and in our day, Sartre has added that "as soon as man apprehends himself as free and wishes to use his freedom . . . then his activity is play." More recently, it has been suggested by several play researchers and theorists that the imaginative character of playful behavior contributes to the development and facilitation of divergent thinking and problem–solving abilities (Ellis, 1973, Lieberman, 1977, Piaget, 1962, Sutton–Smith, 1966). Additionally, "**playfulness**" has been directly correlated with generalized thinking ability, complex symbolization, higher levels of analytical conceptual thinking, creativity, imagination, fantasy, intelligence, reading comprehension, mathematical skills, verbal skills, novel strategizing, flexibility, fluency, intimacy, inclusion, risk–taking, cooperation, and higher levels of trust (Hutt and Bhavnani, 1972, Horne and Philleo, 1942, Wallach and Kogan, 1965, Wign, Gould, Yeates and Brierly, 1977, McCall, 1974, Fink, 1976, Lovingen, 1974, Smilansky, 1968, Wolfgang, 1974, Humphrey, 1965, 1966, Zammarelli and Bolton, 1977, Feitelson and Ross, 1973, Golomb and Cornelius, 1977, Gunn 1978, 1980, 1981, 1982, Kleiber, 1979, and Ellis, 1973).

In Ashley Montagu's new book, *Growing Young*, he convincingly argues that human beings are not meant to grow old, but rather to fulfill their childhood by maturing such youthful traits as curiosity, imaginativeness, honestly, questioning, playfulness, open–mindedness, flexibility, humor, willingness to experiment, receptivity to new ideas, eagerness to learn and spontaneity. Montagu masterfully assembles historical, anthropological and psychological evidence that adults of our species are meant to be in an unending state of "childhood development." That is, we as human beings in body, spirit, feeling, and conduct are designed to grow and develop in ways that emphasize rather than minimize childhood traits. We are intended to remain, in many ways,

46 CHALLENGE OF EXCELLENCE

playful. We were never intended to grow up into the kind of adults most of us have become. His overall thesis contends that biologically, human beings are characterized by "neoteny" (from 'neos' = youthful, 'teino' = to extend forward), the extension into adult life of childhood characteristics. He contends that our current "adultishness" causes us to develop "psychosclerosis" — hardening of the mind.

Psychologist Mihaly Csikszenthmihal has demonstrated repeatedly that we have available to us increased resources in this state of "playfulness" which he characteristically calls "flow." In a state of "flow" we undergo an intense centering of attention on the activity. We do not "try to concentrate harder, the concentration comes automatically." Concentration is like breathing — it isn't even considered. By some it is said, "My concentration is complete. My mind isn't wandering. I'm not thinking about something else. I'm totally involved in what I'm doing. My body feels good and awake all over. My energy is flowing smoothly. I'm relaxed, comfortable, and energetic." For some there is a sense of "being lost in the action. My sense of time is altered." Ted Williams said he could sometimes see the seams turning on a ball that was approaching him at ninety miles per hour. Csikszenthmihalyi goes on to argue that this state of "flow" can be induced by presenting an individual with activity that allows an individual to meet a challenge at the outer limits of their ability. It is these "outer limits" that are tested and tapped by the EXCELLENCE PRINCIPLE™. If volumes of research support the positive correlation between "playfulness" and highly valued social and professional skills, it seems only logical that states of playfulness can be used to teach and enhance the primary communication skills necessary for professional success.

I had long known the value of "playfulness" as an internal *resource state*. However, prior to extensive training in NeuroLinguistic Programming I had no consistent "struc-

The Play Frame 47

ture or "model" to understand the syntax of the behavior. Through the utilization of NLP I was able to study the "structure" of peak performances, and have consistently found that "FUN IS A PREREQUISITE TO EXCELLENCE," play is the behavior of enlightenment. The **"Challenge of Excellence"** asks each participant to stretch the boundaries of their imagination, flexibility, sensory awareness, creativity, and conceptual thinking through participation in adult "gaming" and "play." Trainees are asked to maximize the resources they had as children in order to elevate their level of performance as adults. More than their heads are involved in learning; their whole bodies are involved.

Current brain research reveals that all stimuli is first coded in the limbic system, and is responsible for emotions and feeling tones. In terms of an NLP model, this means that we first understand information through our kinesthetic senses. This may account for "intuition." In the past it was generally assumed that we could "change our feelings by changing our thoughts." The *reverse* now appears to be true. "We can change the way in which we think by changing our movement and feelings (or our body)." The EXCELLENCE PRINCIPLE tests this presupposition.

THE EXCELLENCE PRINCIPLE

PRESUPPOSITIONS:

- ANY PROBLEM CAN BE COLLAPSED IF THE **RESOURCE STATE** IS POWERFUL ENOUGH.
- THE **KINESTHETIC** PORTION OF INTERNAL EXPERIENCE IS THE **MOST POWERFUL** COMPONENT OF HUMAN EXPERIENCE.
- THE **PHYSIOLOGY** OF EXCELLENCE CAN OFFER BOUNTIFUL RESOURCES FOR ALL FACETS OF LIFE.
- **PLAYFULNESS, FUN, CHALLENGE,** AND **CELEBRATION** ARE POWERFUL **UNIVERSAL** RESOURCE STATES WITH MULTI–FACETED RESOURCES: THE "**ELIXIR PLEXUS**"™ OF LIFE.
- FRAMING CHANGE WORK IN **FUN** IS ELEGANT AND STREAMLINED.
- MOST CHANGE WORK MOVES TOWARD **ENJOYMENT** AS A COMPONENT OF DESIRED STATE. THE **"CHALLENGE OF EXCELLENCE"** BEGINS IN **ENJOYMENT**. CHANGE WORK CAN BE FUN!
- LEARNING IS MAXIMIZED WHEN WE HAVE ALREADY HAD THE EXPERIENCE THAT RELATES TO WHAT WE READ OR HEAR ABOUT.
- ACCESS"**ELIXIR PLEXUS**"™ = **FULL** UTILIZATION OF RESOURCES = **PEAK** PERFORMANCE AND **MAXIMUM** PRODUCTIVITY.

The Play Frame 49

Learning is framed in "play" (The Play Frame). Within the PLAY FRAME individuals' strategies will be maximized. Through the calibration skills inherent in the Excellence Principle of NLP, we are able to actually code the "formula" for personal successes, and offer the formula to participants as a way to "solve problems" in other areas of their lives.

The most OFTEN REPEATED "STREAMLINED" STRATEGY FOR SUCCESS that we've calibrated over and over is:

$$K \longrightarrow A^i_F \longrightarrow V^c_{ie} I$$

When presented with a task the person accesses a K lead (accesses the information first coded in the limbic system as a <u>feeling</u> tone or vibrational frequency). they listen for their "familiar voice" (a distinctly different tonality from all the other 300,000 tonal distinctions we are capable of coding) — in Native American culture this **familiar voice** or **true voice** is the heart voice of the unconscious mind that always instructs and commands but never forbids. We've noted over and over again that this "true voice" is attached to **feelings** or a K lead, is about a middle C in pitch, is **felt** from the heart region, is encouraging and enthusiastic, and often whispers. The "true voice" sends into "up time" by visually attending in the integrated construction mode. That is, a person begins filming what is actually happening at the moment. In this highly integrated state, what is seen is immediately felt again and the true voice continues to instruct. This loop seems to be the strategy for being **centered** or **living in the moment**.

Challenge, fun, playfulness, and adventure are powerful universal resource states with multiple resources for success. *Playfulness is the behavior of enlightenment.* By **tapping** these resource states, we seek to tap the "ELIXIR PLEXUS"™ of experience. (Figure 12)

THE EXCELLENCE PRINCIPLE

- Any problem can be integrated into a RESOURCE STATE if the resource state is powerful enough.
- The KINESTHETIC portion of internal experience is the most powerful component of human experience. The body must run a pattern for the nervous system to be programmed to utilize the pattern.
- The PHYSIOLOGY of excellence can offer bountiful resources for all facets of life.
- PLAYFULNESS, FUN, CHALLENGE, and CELEBRATION are powerful UNIVERSAL resource states with multi–faceted resources: The ELIXIR PLEXUS™ of life.
- Framing change in FUN and challenge is elegant and streamlined, and accesses the best of our child, . . . our dreamer.

ELIXIR PLEXUS™

"THE PURE, CONCENTRATED ESSENCE
OF ANYTHING"

"THE <u>MOST PERFECT MANIFESTATION</u> OR
<u>EMBODIMENT</u> OF A QUALITY OR THING"

- PEAK PERFORMANCE !

- RESPONSE A !

- THRESHOLD TO EXCELLENCE !

FIGURE 12

52 CHALLENGE OF EXCELLENCE

By accessing these powerful resource states through the Play Frame and the Excellence Principle, we have opportunity to utilize these states to promote human excellence. Access to the "Elixir Plexus" leads to full utilization of resources, which leads to peak performances and maximum productivity, which leads to self love, and love of others. People who PLAY together LOVE each other, . . . and that's what all of us are really about, after all.

"If happiness is activity in accordance with excellence, it is reasonable that it should be in accordance with the highest excellence."

Aristotle

7

TAKING IT HOME

There are many wonderful adventure and challenge programs in existence, and we've had the opportunity both to experience and work with some of them. We are often asked, "Is what you do like Outward Bound?" Our response is "What we do is BEYOND Outward Bound. The only similarity is that we offer challenge experiences." Our UTILIZATION of challenge experiences is what lends extreme uniqueness to the **"Challenge of Excellence."**

It has been our observation that many challenge experiences stand as isolated moments in a person's life . . . a vacation or trip to remember, but somehow unrelated to personal relationships or professional work patterns. This is where we are MARKEDLY DIFFERENT. We insure that the patterns elicited and installed are directly connected to the "real world" of everyday experience.

The technology used is called "future pacing" or "taking it home." The actual maneuver is a simple one already discussed as a "collapsed reality." We simply continue to

54 CHALLENGE OF EXCELLENCE

"**collapse into**" or **connect** elegant body patterns to personal and professional situations. TIMING the connection and *utilizing a word* that MEANS a specific situation or set of circumstances becomes the art form of sculpting excellence.

Timing a connection when a person is running an elegant body pattern that cannot change once achieved is most useful. This is why we love the three story balance beams, or our five story zip line platform, or our four story pamper pole. When a body is perfectly balanced on an eleven inch square platform or fully extended in space — flying — it will remain so no matter what "psychological problem" or difficulty a person is forced to recall as a result of our shouting reminders.

We recall an alcoholic woman who would not tolerate a discussion of her mother. It always "knocked her off balance;" she quit breathing, numbed herself, and drank. Our challenge was to interrupt this pattern firmly established in her nervous system and install a pattern of balance and full breathing in the face of "mother". The pamper pole was the perfect place to do this. When standing four stories high on an eleven inch square platform the body is highly motivated to stand tall and balanced. The body is also breathing fully and powerfully in order to sustain the balance. We take such elegant moments to **rewire** the nervous system for success. By using a statement as simple as, "What would your MOTHER think of you now?" forces our player to access all the old **shut down** patterns associated with "mother." Only this time it's different. The nervous system is forced to **connect tall, balanced,** and **breathing** to "mother." This obviously changes her entire experience of "mother". She literally can no longer respond the same. The word "mother" now triggers her to stand tall, square up, and breath fully. We're convinced that such a posture allows "mother" to perceive our player differently and thus respond differently. It's a law of system analysis: If you change ANY part of a system, you change the total system! TIMING the connection to an irreversible moment of excellence and gathering enough information so as to have KEY WORDS to elicit computer programs of life is the secret to insuring that folks take the experience home.

It is also important to double check the connection once the player is on the ground. This can be done by simply saying, "Well, what WOULD your mother think of you now?" Punch out or accent the word "mother" since it's what pulls up all her old patterns or programs of "mother." If the new neurological pathway is made, what you'll see is something like this: she'll immediately stand tall, square up, breath a deep breath, and probably reply "who gives a damn what she thinks?" This response opens our player to **walk her own path** rather than drown her despair in alcohol.

We personally like to insure the pattern is well embedded so we're very likely to have her enact a **coup** on a "mother" image of an opposing clan during the game of Indian Coup. Repeated demonstrations of the new pattern associated with "mother" insures us that any contact with "mother" in the future will serve to remind her of her own excellence . . . a moment in time when she succeeded. Future pacing insures that the "highs" of challenge experiences form bridges to paths of daily excellence. Now let's look at the specifics of the Challenge Course and how we use it.

56 CHALLENGE OF EXCELLENCE

PART II

58 CHALLENGE OF EXCELLENCE

8

WELCOME TO THE CHALLENGE OF EXCELLENCE

Imagine yourself driving over miles of rolling green hills, freckled with country ponds and small lakes. Hereford cattle and quarter horses dot the hillsides, and great condors and redtailed hawks glide in spiraling circles on the sunlit wind. The breeze always blows in Oklahoma, bringing a welcomed coolness to the warm summer days. Majestic cottonwood trees cool and sing to the valleys and ponds on the ranch. Black Jack, Oak, Hickory, and Elm grace the hill tops. The sky is perpetually blue, painted with explosive white clouds, and the sunrises and sunsets are breath–taking. The orchards blossom with peach, apple, cherries, plums, and pears in the spring.

The summer garden supplies much of the campers' food. Dome tents and tepees preserve the rustic atmosphere and simplicity we so enjoy.

The Broken Spoke Ranch, Home of Excellence Unlimited, Inc. and The Magical Child Foundation, is surrounded by five huncred acres of rolling green lands and forests. It is located seventy miles from the geographic center of the USA. Campers from around the world come to take the "Challenge of Excellence" and most are surprised at the beauty of the land and the warmth of the people. Come with us through the portals of "change" to take the Challenge of Excellence.

62 CHALLENGE OF EXCELLENCE

9

INITIATION TO LEARNING THE ROPES

A friendly, relaxed and playful atmosphere is fertile ground for growth, change, and tapping human excellence. We begin our first day on the ropes playing together, loosening up, finding our balance, and perfecting our breathing.

BREATHING is the single most important component of excellence. Only as our life force flows easily and steadily through us can we use the body to experience our essence. We begin by learning to BREATHE deep into our abdomen, pulling air up through our chest and backs, expanding fully and exhaling easily. Any good yoga or Feldenkrais lesson would be appropriate here.

BREATHING LESSON

A few simple things you can do to increase awareness of breathing and thus improve that function are these: have folks lie down on their backs and notice their breathing, whether the breaths are large or small, whether they

64 CHALLENGE OF EXCELLENCE

breathe mostly in their chest or abdomen, etc. No change is required and no one way is "right"; they are just exploring, paying attention. Have them rest their hand on their abdomen, and draw breaths in below their navel to form a little football there, continuing that movement gently many times. Then after a short rest, have them put their hand on their chest and draw breath into the upper chest, lifting it up toward the ceiling and up toward their chins. Do this many times. Then have them alternate, once in the abdomen, once in the upper chest. Rest. Next, have them reach beside themselves with both hands on their lower ribs and expand those ribs out with their breath many times. During a brief rest, in which they just relax, breathe normally, have them become aware of any changes in the way or amount they breathe. Now ask them to bring their knees up, feet on the floor, and use their breath to press their lower back to the ground. As they do this many times, remind them that the lungs don't have muscle tissue, so that it is the opening of the space around them that allows them to fill. They are like a balloon, and will expand anywhere the space is provided. Tell them not to keep their balloon flat in the back. Ask them to roll on their stomach and breathe big breaths into their back, then roll on their back and feel their entire back pressing the floor as it expands in breathing. Finally, have them breathe in a relaxed manner and notice that their breath is probably fuller and easier. When you say "breathe" today, this kind of openness and ease is possible and desirable. Thus we insure that each camper can breathe properly and is anchored to the signal "Breathe"!

There are three physiological states always present during peak performances:

1. The heart region is expanded, open, and directly over or in front of the buttocks.

2. The eyes are soft and moist, allowing full and deep

Initiation To Learning The Ropes 65

vision.

3. The individual is breathing fully and constantly, with ease.

We call the combination of these, "The Excellence Posture." It is a free moving, easeful way of being in our bodies. Each player is asked to model this posture.

Next we practice BALANCE on the balls of the feet, the "heart spot" in reflexology. The Excellence Posture and balancing on the Heart Spot are considered to be basic to maximizing the benefits of the Ropes Course.

66 CHALLENGE OF EXCELLENCE

For this, have the players stand, feet about as wide apart as their shoulders to give them a good foundation. Then, ask them to pay attention to how they are standing on their feet. Are they resting back on their heels with their knees locked, or do they stand on the outside of their feet, are they on the balls of their feet? Now, have them raise themselves up onto the balls of their feet and lightly down, continuing this movement in an easy manner, spending more and more time balancing on the balls of their feet as they proceed. Have them notice that this automatically brings their heart a bit up and forward if they allow it. Remind them to breathe freely and openly as they move, giving them the pattern of breathing when they are concentrating on a new task. Once they have this and have rested briefly, let them do this again, but more freely now, like a gentle bouncing, which can become a bouncy step back and forth between the left and right feet. Then the feet can move and dance around, much like a boxer dancing around an opponent. Let the players know that it is from this spot that they can move *any* direction they want without extra preparation — they have the most freedom this way. To emphasize that, have them stand way back on their heels, or slouched onto the sides of their feet, and notice that they need to spend time rolling up to balance on the balls of the feet before they can take action. Why not keep that spot under us all the time? One more thing that will be useful is to talk with them about tensing their feet, which they may unconsciously do on a difficult element. Have them walk around with their feet tense, tight, and gripped. It will be very quickly obvious that this makes progress difficult even on smooth ground; they certainly will not want to do this when in a challenging situation. If they notice they are doing it, have them stop a moment, breathe and find easy balance on relaxed feet.

Balance and the Heart Spot

Next we feel that it's important to play with people, laugh together, and get to know each other like we did as kids. When people play they will access their very finest strategies of excellence because they are free of stress and requirements to perform "correctly."

The *New Games* book is a great resource for warmup games that are fun and non–threatening. Games that give them patterns of cooperation, that remind them of being

68 CHALLENGE OF EXCELLENCE

a kid, that get them running and breathing freely, that create laughter, that have them touch each other are all great as warm–ups. Get them laughing, cheering and alive.

This is a place where some programs add a few stretching exercises as warmups. These are wonderful, *and* we want to add a note of caution here. Many of the players have not stretched or exercised much lately. If you give them any drastic stretches, it is very easy for them to overdo it in the excitement and pressure of the group situation. This creates strains and sprains which then make their ropes course days tougher. Be sure to be gentle, allow them their own pace and ease. Before they begin is a great time to be clear with them about paying attention to themselves, finding improvement through ease and enjoyment rather than through effort and strain.

Three or four introductory games are sufficient to relax the group and allow them to know each other. We then prepare them to "support" each other on the course.

SPOTTING

The low elements of the challenge course are potentially the most dangerous. Unlike the high elements, safety and support depends on each other rather than a mechanical safety system. Each of the elements require that the group know how to support each others' weight and block a fall. The following exercises are helpful to teach "spotting."

GROUND TRUST FALL. Two players of approximately the same size pair up. One stands a few feet behind the other. The front player spreads their arms and falls backward, stiff into the arms of their partner. The partner catches them under the arms. This is repeated a few times, each with increasingly greater distance. This can also be done with two supporters catching, as in this picture.

70 CHALLENGE OF EXCELLENCE

SPOTTING HIGH. We use the "Drunk Walk" to teach the group to *Spot High* on the body. The group forms two lines and a member of the players performs a clumsy walk down the middle. The group breaks their falls by catching them under the arms or at chest level and returns them to a standing position. Learning to expect the unexpected is essential in spotting.

ARM SUPPORT. "The Cookie Toss" is a fun way to teach the group how to catch the weight of a falling body.

Initiation To Learning The Ropes 71

The group lines up facing each other with arms bent at the elbows and inter-spaced without touching. A player runs and leaps into the arms of the group while yelling their favorite cookie. The group catches the player and bounces them down the line, turning "the cookie over" midpoint.

The group is now relaxed, breathing, and ready to support each other through the low elements.

72 CHALLENGE OF EXCELLENCE

10

THE LOW ELEMENTS

The "Challenge of Excellence" ropes course was built by **Timothy G. Kempfe** of **Adventure Experiences.** We enthusiastically recommend him and his team of builders.

Adventure Experiences
Rt. 2, Box 24K–6
Trinity, Texas 75862
(409) 594–2541 Office
(409) 594–2945 Home

74 CHALLENGE OF EXCELLENCE

The low elements are:

The Trust Fall

The Swinging Log

76 CHALLENGE OF EXCELLENCE

The Track Walk or Balance Beam

The Triangular Traverse

The Low Elements 77

The Wild Woosey

The Kitten Crawl

78 CHALLENGE OF EXCELLENCE

The Swinging Tires

The Fidget Ladder

The Low Elements 79

The Flea Hop

The Hickory Jump

The Log Jam

Each low element will now be discussed individually for the patterns that it elicits and the patterns that are installed by its use. Before introducing each element for its specific use, we would like to introduce the basic movement patterns that are easily detected on both the high and low elements. These are the basic patterns of *tracking excellence* and can be detected in all types of activities.

11

PATTERNS OF THE MIND MIRRORED BY THE BODY

Remember, whatever pattern is modeled in the body is the exact pattern that is available to the mind. The body **mirrors** the messages coded on the nervous system. The muscles and bones can only do what they are programmed to do. The following are the most common patterns we see and are the basis for our offering other "choices."

1. *Clinging to Support From Behind.* Those players who hang on to support from behind are often those who depend on their *past experiences* as a reference for the present and future. In a work setting they will often be less flexible and more dependent. They will be less creative than the person who envisions what can be done in the future.

2. *Refusing Assistance.* The player who automatically pulls away from the spotters is not accustomed to receiving support and will often take on too big of a load. Assistance is often coded as a failure, which denies cooperation and slows down the process of achieving an outcome. Those who refuse assistance will often "assist" others when it isn't necessary and thus deny others their own talents.

Patterns of the Mind Mirrored by the Body

3. *Beginning a Task Without Establishing an Outcome.* A majority of people are not automatic and fluid goal–setters. Most people's experience in education has taught them to go inside themselves and "discuss" the task at hand, rather than quiet themselves, eyeball the outcome desired, and move steadily toward it. Those who haven't learned to establish an outcome for themselves right up front will immediately look down at their feet to find their balance, rather than allowing their feet to *feel* balance in relation to where they are headed. Sometimes people will "look *beyond*" their outcome by holding their heads too high. Both of these movements disregard the outcome as important and program the body to fail in the task.

4. *Hesitation and False Starts.* Persons who wait a long time to begin the element, or who start and stop several times, utilize the same pattern in their personal and professional lives. It is important to get a person to initiate and complete the element without hesitation and false starts. It is helpful to get the person to experience being at the other end of the task and "feeling" the good feeling of completion and success.

5. *Rigidity.* Persons who perform the elements with rigidity and jerkiness do the same in real life. They are prone to be inflexible in decision–making and often snappy or angry if things don't go their way. Teaching a body to relax and move with grace and ease also teaches a mind to "lighten up" and enjoy more choices. Often much body work is required to *relax* a truly rigid body. However, the end result of emotional ease and flexibility is worth the investment of time.

6. *Condemning Oneself.* When players fall off balance and immediately snarl, shake their heads "no," curse, etc. they very likely learned early on that "mistakes" were unacceptable. Those who can't fall off balance, giggle or smile, and regain their balance are those who will take very few risks. If *failure* is unacceptable then their *taking a risk* is unacceptable. Those who beat themselves for "falling off balance" will waste enormous amounts of time griping, will rarely complete tasks successfully, and will deter others from achieving success by condemning them in the same way. Staff morale around such a person will be low. The habits of the nervous system are the habits of life. Ask this person to *positively coach* themselves through the elements, i.e. "I'm gaining my balance and moving forward, slowly. I'm relaxing my feet and hands. I'm breathing and seeing exactly where I am going," etc.

7. *Falling Over the Finish Line.* These are the players who move slowly toward an outcome until the very end when they "hurry up" and fall. They will increase their speed at the end of the element and *lunge* for the outcome or end. They, of course, lose their balance and complete the task *out–of–control.* They will often experience last minute disappointment in their lives.

We make the analogy of stalking a rabbit. The hunter may stalk quietly, gracefully, patiently, but if at the last minute he lunges with the rabbit stick to make the kill, the rabbit is likely to sprint away unharmed! The hunt was good, but the kill unsuccessful. We teach our players to "come lightly to the finish and touch the outcome gently in complete control."

Patterns of the Mind Mirrored by the Body 87

8. *Looking Away From the Outcome.* Often times players will establish *eye–level* contact with the outcome, but look away when spoken to, or when they arrive at a new and different point on the elements. Most often they will immediately lose balance. The body is programmed by our focus. If the eyes look down to the side, the body receives a message to turn downward and to the side. If the eyes look way up, the body thinks it should try to move *up*. Maintaining a steady focus on the outcome (with soft eyes) keeps the body moving steadily in that direction. This principle is true for walking a balance beam as well as achieving a corporate outcome for increased productivity.

88 CHALLENGE OF EXCELLENCE

9. *Allowing External Input to Alter Intention.* Persons who alter their direction based on the input or opinion of others will most often be unaware of their own life goals, and will experience fatigue and frustration over their attempts to adjust their direction to suit others. These will lose their balance when they hear a loud noise or will focus their eyes on the audience when beginning a task. They will also turn their eyes away from their outcome to listen to the comments or instruction of others. Each time they move their eyes to look at whoever is speaking, they lose their balance. They are also unable to find their balance to initiate a task in the beginning because they are looking at others. They will also get a facial flush tone change to bright red or increased warmth each time they lose their balance.

Patterns of the Mind Mirrored by the Body 89

Utilize their attachment to external stimuli by softly insisting that they keep their eyes focused on their outcome. It may be necessary to position oneself at the point of the outcome to **coach** them toward their goal. This is an excellent time to **suggest** that they consider using this position to do what they want to do, versus always following the advice of others. These players can learn to assume the "excellence posture" and integrate the opinions of others with their own without changing their focus of attention.

10. *The "Start–Stop" Pattern.* These folks will begin a task and then literally "stop in mid–air." They seem to be able to initiate a task, but the feeling of movement is immediately interrupted. The nervous system apparently got the message to **expect** interruption. Often this pattern of "start–stop" is installed very young, i.e., a child is playing and is jerked or suddenly snatched up by a parent or teacher. This pattern in the nervous system means that they will rarely be able to complete tasks and when they do they will have used far more energy than most because they've had to "start up" again and again and again. It's useful to gently assist this person by helping balance them to *keep a roll going.* Their bodies must experience the feeling of moving *un*interrupted before the mind can do so.

11. *Going Without Commitment.* These are the players who are constantly doing (or going through the motions of doing) what they don't want to do. They will initiate a task without being ready. They may step or jump onto an element, and begin without establishing an outcome or finding their balance. They may also be seen to nod "no" or "shrug" with non–committal just before beginning. *Stop* them immediately and insist they *get ready.* While they're "getting ready" suggest to them to do the same all the time.

90 CHALLENGE OF EXCELLENCE

12. *Rushing to do a Task Before the Support System is in Place.* These players rush to do an activity before the spotters are ready. They will often be one who feels or actually is deserted by friends and family. They will feel bad because nobody is supportive of them. They most often don't realize that this happens because they rush so fast that their support is left behind. *SLOW THEM DOWN* and request that they ask the spotters, "Are you ready?" Ask them to gently, but firmly, command the spotters' attention. Only when all are attending to the task can real progress be made. This simple pattern installation can actually change the entire way in which a player relates to family, friends, and colleagues.

Patterns of the Mind Mirrored by the Body 91

13. *Always Going First, Last, Etc.* If you observe that certain players go *first* on two or more elements, challenge them to go last, or third, or a variety of positions. *TWICE IS A PATTERN!* When you see a pattern two or more times you may know that the person has a **habit** of running the observed pattern. Challenge them to try another pattern in order to *add multiple choices* to their behavior. Players who always go first will rarely be aware of others. They go first, get finished, and *space out* (literally or figuratively). They are unable to observe patterns of excellence or failure in others and learn from them. They are limited only to what they know and can gather by themselves. By asking them to "wait" and "observe," they will automatically have more choices of behavior. Likewise, players who always go last will be unable to perform without models

92 CHALLENGE OF EXCELLENCE

and support. This means, very simply, that they will be unable to "follow their own hunches and ideas." Challenge them to go first several times in order to give the nervous system the message of moving immediately with an idea. *ENLIGHTENMENT* is the ability to act spontaneously. There is no lag time between conceiving an idea and acting upon it. To offer one the opportunity to have this experience in their nervous system is to make "enlightenment" possible for them.

If certain players always *wait until last* they will diminish the value of their own ideas and will always be *comparing* in order to judge the value of themselves. Our personal worth can not be compared to anyone else. We are each unique and need to have experiences that insure us the value of sharing our uniqueness. *Going first* gives the nervous system this message.

14. *Overshooting or Undershooting a Mark.* Players who leap, and either overshoot or undershoot their mark, can never be satisfied. They can never get what they want. Those who *overshoot* their mark will often start a task by looking up and out into space. When the eyes look out into space, the body is programmed to move there. What is up and out beyond is *imagined* and never the same as what is here and now . . . or eye–level. To "imagine and dream" successfully is to *intend the essence of the outcome,* not the *form!* However, if one is always "looking beyond," the body tries to go there. For example, if a person looks up into the trees when trying to balance, the body loses full feeling of being in contact with the balance log. Thus, the person will fall off balance. They will also be prone to physical pain, accident, or illness because they're not in "touch" with their feeling body. They will "fall off balance" the same way psychologically.

The principle of a body going for what it sees is also true of the one who "falls short of the mark." Take the time to help people focus softly on their outcome. This insures that the body accesses exactly what is needed for the task; no more, and no less. This equals maximum utilization of energy.

15. *Walking Heavy.* Those who stomp hard or walk **heavy** are those who *stomp hard* on others or themselves and are prone to carrying a heavy load . . . either their own or others. Getting them to "walk lightly" is an easeful way to program their brain to "lighten up" and unload some of the necessary baggage of responsibility. Those who walk heavy are the type of managers who will be "hard" on others and will be unable to inspire excitement and good morale. Do everything possible to get them to *walk lightly.*

For the "heavy walkers" who step back, tuck their chin a bit, or tighten up when asked to "walk lightly" (this response is known as a *polarity response*), it may be useful to have them carry an additional load across the elements, i.e. a backpack full of rocks. Hopefully, as they *shed* the rocks they will feel the meaning of "lightening up." Their heads will never understand this meaning until their bodies do! Ridding themselves of unnecessary responsibility will be a joy to them and everyone around them.

16. *Needing an Audience.* These are the players who will check to make sure everyone is watching before they begin a task, rather than spending this time establishing an outcome. Only when the outcome is established by literally seeing where they are going can the "performance" be successful. This is the player whose performance leaves much to be desired, but the initial expectation was high. Challenge this person to look softly at their outcome to initiate a task and take their bows *after* the performance rather than before. The players who concentrate on the performance and then takes their bows usually have something to bow over.

17. *Recovery Strategies.* We all seek balance. This is be-

cause we're constantly being knocked off balance. To be knocked off balance is natural. This is why it's important to have recovery strategies. The person with poor recovery strategies will be stiff in the legs, neck, elbows, hands, spine, hips, and/or shoulders. *A STIFF BODY EQUALS A STIFF MIND!* Mind and body are one. To understand the mind of a person, learn to read their body! Persons who are flexible in their body will easily move to adjust when knocked off balance. Stiff or *inflexible persons* will not be able to complete most of the tasks without assistance. This principle holds true for their lives! If certain players continue to fall off balance or require support on an element due to inflexibility, remove them from the element and relax them through a breathing exercise, massage, or the very elegant use of Feldenkrais movement. They cannot be flexible in their minds if their bodies are inflexible!

Patterns of the Mind Mirrored by the Body 95

Remember that the most successful people play games and sports that require movement! In professions where risks are required, it is essential to have good recovery strategies! Learning to regain one's balance on a swinging log or balance beam will recode one's nervous system to recover when emotionally thrown a curve.

18. *Blaming*. Players who can fall off balance and immediately smile rather than frown and curse themselves are guaranteed to get what they want *more quickly*. If they smile and lighten up immediately, they are free to re-focus their outcome and keep moving. If they frown and condemn themselves, they will spend valuable time griping and complaining rather than remembering *where they were going*. The same is true for those who are observed to point their finger and curse *the element* when they fall off balance. This is a neurological pattern. It's a habit in their

96 CHALLENGE OF EXCELLENCE

bodies. They, therefore, must do it a lot. If, when players fail, they blame someone or something outside themselves, they'll not be able to re–center themselves and re–establish their outcome. Challenge them to *smile* all the way through the task and particularly when they fall off balance.

19. *Not Able to Hang On.* These are the players who are able to jump for an outcome, i.e., a trapeze, but are unable to hold on. Often times they will have the trapeze firmly in their hand, but they let go and fall. These are the same players who often come in contact with what they want but can't sustain the behavior to actually hang on what they want. If the body doesn't believe it can have what it wants, neither does the mind.

Challenge these players to hang on even if they need to be supported. We will often chunk the task down small enough for gradual success. For example, rather than trying to leap out and grab and hang on to a trapeze, we may have the player hang from a bar slightly above their reach. After their bodies understand how to hang on while holding their weight, they can attempt to leap and hang on. The players who learn to hold on to what they get will be far more motivated to *go for outcomes* than those who never experience "holding on."

20. *Supporting One's Own Weight.* We often see people who are considered to be overweight. We only consider this to be a problem if it affects their *balance, lightness,* and *agility.* Anyone who is too heavy to *lift their own weight* up a ladder, or support their own weight while hanging from a bar *cannot* support their own weight in a family or organization. They may appear to carry more of the weight, but they, in fact, carry responsibilities that others could do better. As long as they carry the responsibilities that are not theirs, there is no space for others to operate. These players usually consider themselves strong supports of others, and are shocked to discover that the message of

Patterns of the Mind Mirrored by the Body 97

their body is *literal* — "They can't support their own weight." We're convinced that a body will often gain this kind of weight just to get the person's attention. It's essential in any group that we be able to *support our own weight.* This is true balance in the layer circle of life.

21. *Avoiding Help.* These are the folks who when touched or supported in any way literally draw back, flinch, or cringe. Their nervous system is coded to disassociate from assistance. In their minds, these people will code *help* as failure and they are usually driven to "try harder." They are our "efforters"! If the body believes that to be helped is to fail, a player is forced to carry an enormous load *all the time.* Such people will be unable to function elegantly on any team. If they code "help as failure" they will be unable to be cooperative and will waste valuable time worrying about themselves when they do need help, rather than exerting this energy focusing on the outcome. They will also be the kind of players who are always "starting over" each time they fail at something, rather than re–adjusting and moving on. To constantly start over is extremely wasteful, so they will tend to be *wasteful . . .* unable to utilize what is available to help them. Intend to assist them through all the elements until their bodies get accustomed to being supported. For fun, we often play "shrink" with these players. This is to have them walk around on their knees like little people. This is a funny and fun way to *have* to get help. They're simply too short to reach things. When the body learns to receive help it learns to receive love and can experience abundance. It is also available to learn the power of the yin (the feminine), which is receptive to higher vibrations that some call intuition!

22. *Life is Serious.* Often we observe players who are *unable to smile* while concentrating on a task. They can laugh before and after, but not during the process. These same players tend to believe that work is serious business.

98 CHALLENGE OF EXCELLENCE

When they tighten their face, they tighten their bodies and invariably lose their balance. The same is true in life. Challenge these folks to maintain a smile while operating (or performing a task). They will be surprised at their improved balance and flexibility, both on the elements and in their lives.

23. *Hurry Up and Finish.* Some players hurry throughout a task. Then they lunge for the final outcome and stumble and lose their balance. They finish the final course "out-of-control." To lose control just prior to getting an outcome is to end up dissatisfied and often empty-handed. Basically, these players perform well and still get limited rewards. We often tell these players that they "scare their prey away."

Challenge these folks to come softly, gently, slowly all the way to the finish. "Touch your heart's desire softly." When we hurry, we lose control. "Slow down, come easy."

24. *Moving Forward Completely Out–of–Control.* These are players who hop up on the elements and tear across it completely out–of–control. Getting to the outcome is a matter of luck rather than skill. It's highly unlikely that these players can get their outcome *repeatedly,* and they definitely can't teach others how to get an outcome. Often times this pattern lets us know that a person is a high risk–taker, but with limited success. They often dream of outcomes far in the future without the experience of re–focusing on the here–and–now which allows them to take the steps to achieve their dreams. Their eyes see only the outcome and their bodies are programmed to race for what they see. *Slow them down* so they can learn to dance life with poise, grace, and self–assured control.

25. *Getting An Outcome is Tuff!* Here come the ole'bottom lip biters. Their teeth are clenched. They grunt, groan, and effort enormously. Most often their bodies are hunched over. If they run this "efforting pattern" on two or more elements, it's a habit and they probably believe that *efforting* and hard work are always necessary in order to get what they want. It's a change of a very old and basic belief system for a player to understand that difficult and challenging tasks can be performed with *ease*. We strongly encourage these players to get involved in activities like akido, graceful forms of dance, Chinese wands, Feldenkrais, etc. We often have them tell a joke or sing an easeful song (like 'Summer Time') while they perform tasks. This re-codes the nervous system to relax and enjoy the experience.

Patterns of the Mind Mirrored by the Body 101

26. *Lip Biting, Shaking the Head No, Tight Lips.* These are all clues that the players are talking to themselves and what they are saying is "negative" or "not useful." The body and the mind are one — twins. What one does the other must do. If the head is saying "No, you can't do this. You're going to fail," the body obliges. When people come to realize this, they can pay more conscious attention to their internal chatter. It seems that most of the time this internal chatter occurs out–of–consciousness. That is to say the player is paying attention to something else besides the chatter. All suggestions about being "enlightened," "self–actualized," etc., insist that internal chatter must be quieted. Have this player stop such talking inside by either singing or talking out loud (where you as the observer have the opportunity to challenge negative chatter). We often say, "BE WILLING TO LIVE WHAT YOU SAY," because our words direct our bodies toward our own reality. We get exactly what we talk about! Thus, use words that speak your heart's desire.

102 CHALLENGE OF EXCELLENCE

27. *Leaning Backward to Move Forward.* It's impossible to find our own balance when we're leaning backward "off balance." When players are leaning back against a tree or post while establishing an outcome of moving forward, the body gets confused and is unable to find its own natural balance. It's impossible to find balance while in a state of imbalance, (in this case a "disassociation"). A player who has a pattern of leaning — on support while getting ready to perform a task will never do the task, or will begin it out–of–control. Challenge the player to stand on their own two feet, breathe, feel their own body, and move forward on their own. Only when these players can stand erect and balanced on their own will they be able to discover and fulfill their heart's desire.

Patterns of the Mind Mirrored by the Body 103

28. *Clinging to Support.* This is the person who grasps and clings tightly to anything close by and refuses to relax their grip and try the task on their own. We think all couples should take the Challenge of Excellence *before* making a marriage or partnership. The person whose body *clings to support* will also *mentally cling* in a relationship. This partnership is bound for unhappiness because neither partner will be able to enjoy the freedom necessary to dance their dreams awake.

We have a special "let go bar" for the "clingers." We simply let them hang from a suspended bar (with their feet a few inches above the ground) until they *have to let go.*

Teaching a body to "let go" is a great gift. My horse, Oklahoma Sunshine Magic, taught me this lesson. When I launched into business on my own I considered all of my

104 CHALLENGE OF EXCELLENCE

assets and what they would be worth to me if I had to liquidate and sell out. As I listed and considered each item, I mentally "let it go." Oklahoma was the only possession I refused to put on my list. I had decided to *keep* her irrespective of the outcome of my business venture. One year later she caught a fatal virus and died. My heart was broken. The only thing I refused to "let go of" was the only thing I LOST!

Help "clingers" to *LET GO* so that they might have what they want in life.

29. *Pulling Back.* Several of our elements require two people to work together . . . to *fully extend themselves* in order to complete the task. The Log Jam and the Wild Woosey are examples. The principle to be learned is that "it requires far less energy to *fully extend* or commit oneself than to *HOLD BACK.*" It is also impossible for one player to succeed without the other. *Both* must *fully extend* themselves. To *pull back* is to *die* in a figurative sense. Everything in nature "grows" or extends beyond the present state. It's unnatural to "pull back" and requires great energy both to pull away and to get going again. To teach a player to "stretch out and extend their body" is to teach them to conserve energy and to cooperate.

106 CHALLENGE OF EXCELLENCE

12

THE LOW ELEMENTS

1. *The Trust Fall. Trust* is essential for achieving excellence, trust in oneself and trust in others. We, therefore, begin with the Trust Fall. We use a 5–6 foot platform. The group is invited to consider silently something that they would love to "trust" having in their experience. Then to avoid long explanations of desired outcomes, we simply have the players "nickname" what they want, i.e., "Blue" for an intimate partnership; "green" for financial abundance; "cloud" for lightness or weight loss; "Tonto" for an improved business partnership. Each member shares their *code word* or nickname for what they want to "trust" having. The group then lines up with their arms extended to support each other. As each member falls and loses balance one line of the group shouts their code word and the other line of the group shouts their name. The technology is simple: the body/mind is being programmed physiologically to "trust" (that is, relax and surrender) having the desired outcome. As the body is actually physiologically falling, the key word to the desired outcome is attached to the mind. In this simple "collapsed reality" the mind is programmed

108 CHALLENGE OF EXCELLENCE

to activate the body to "trust" the desired state. In other words, when the person thinks of "blue," "green," etc. their bodies "relax and surrender." This act of "believing in the body" actually serves to bring the desired state into the players' path.

In the *Trust Fall* it is important that all members do the activity. It is basic to the rest of the course. It is also important that they repeat their performance until they can fall backward, straight (no butt drops!) with their eyes open. The trust fall sets up a cooperative frame among the group members and readies each player to try the other elements.

Utilization. Trust and trustworthiness are synonymous. The player who easily trusts others can also be trusted and is more likely to "dream into existence" that which they "trust" having. It is easy to detect a trusting/trustworthy player. They will easily access a desired state and nickname it. The code word or nickname will be a positive word and said in an enthusiastic tone. When they perform the trust fall they will do so without hesitation and in the proper position.

The person who has difficulty thinking of what they want to trust and what to call it, obviously has little practice in trusting. They will appear stiffer on the ledge, hesitate turning around backward, often make a few false starts before actually falling, and may buckle on the fall. It is important to the rest of the training that they repeat the trust fall until they can do so without hesitation and in good form. This will re–program the body to "trust," which in turn will allow for more emotional trust and flexibility.

The Low Elements 109

2. *The Swinging Log.* The Swinging Log is one of our favorite teachers. Through observing participation on it we are able to detect *how balanced* a player is when the *foundation is shaky* beneath them; how well they *recover*; how they *set* and *maintain an outcome*; how *controlled* they are in getting an outcome; how they *complete a task*; how they *process external information* while performing a task; how they *coach themselves* to completion; how much they *effort* to perform a task; how well they *receive help*; and how *flexible* they are. The patterns a player manifests on the swinging log are the same as those they use when things are shaky beneath them.

Utilization. The well–balanced, integrated player will step lightly onto the log, drop their center of gravity down to balance, pinpoint an outcome at the opposite end of the log — eye level, using their arms and hands to balance — and move in a fluid, floating fashion and maintaining soft eye contact with the outcome while moving gently. They will also make fluid, graceful recoveries and smile at each "off–balancing" movement. External coaching is received

110 CHALLENGE OF EXCELLENCE

and appropriately utilized without obvious impact and diversion from the task. They will come gently and slowly to their outcome, touching it lightly. While they are moving gracefully we talk to them of success in areas that are often "shaky" in their lives.

3. *The Track Walk or Balance Beam.* Our track walk goes up, down, and around. It is excellent for detecting basic patterns of *balance, moving upward, moving downward, setting outcomes, flexibility,* or *re–establishing outcomes* at each point along the way, *response to an audience,* and *utilizing support.*

Utilization. The well–balanced player steps gently and slowly onto the balance beam, drops their center of gravity onto the logs, breathes easily and constantly, focuses on the first point to be reached and goes for the outcome with ease and poise. When a person is able to model independence and balance we talk to them about "bringing into balance those things in their lives which are out of balance," i.e., their work and play, giving and receiving, male and female, leading and following, moving and resting, etc. Often, if we suggest something that is way out of balance in their lives they will fall off balance and have to

The Low Elements 111

recover. We'll continue to repeat this topic until they can walk balanced.

We also use the balance beam to teach people to remain balanced in the face of that which usually "gets their button" or upsets them. We may have them put an imaginary picture of their adversary at the end of the balance beam and have them walk balanced in the face of such a person or situation.

The balance beam is also excellent for teaching a person to walk balanced toward their desired outcome or heart's desire. We simply have them imagine "having what they want at the end of the walk." Such a walk teaches the body to honor the "dreamer" with balance. Our dreamer (or heartful intentions) needs a balanced and graceful mind/body in order to be able to physically manifest our dreams.

112 CHALLENGE OF EXCELLENCE

4. *The Triangle Traverse.* The triangle traverse elicits patterns for *walking the line*, dealing with the *shakes, supporting your own weight,* and *establishing an outcome.* Being able to hold a strong "intention" is also necessary for success.

Utilization. The triangle traverse requires extreme concentration and the ability to target an outcome and hold it constant. Because the wire and the support system is so shaky, it is necessary to fix a point with the eyes and "ride the shakes out" by holding the eyes fixed to a steady point. This is a great element for installing strategies to "walk the line" and "test" one's ability to deal with external stimuli while holding their own intention constant. We often "chatter wildly" while a player is on the triangle traverse. They must keep their own intention strong in order to deal with the shaky wire. We have them move in a complete triangle so that they can move "shaky" forward, backward, and sideways. Maintaining an outcome, softening up, and continuing to move is a useful pattern for meeting deadlines under pressure. "Efforting" and "struggle" result in failure on this element and in most of life.

The Low Elements 113

5. *The Wild Woosey.* *Partnership* is a requirement for this element. Two people must agree to *trust* each other and *cooperate* to achieve the outcome. Both must *fully extend themselves* and *commit* their weight to each other. *Paying attention* to each other, *pacing* each other, and *communicating effectively* are all patterns that are elicited with this element. This activity works best with partners who are *equal* in size and strength. When performed excellently, equal partners smoothly step together onto the wires, fully extend their arms and clasp fingers, extend and straighten their backs, focus their attention on each other's eyes and begin balancing their weight in the middle while moving slowly and positively coaching each other. These body movements are excellent metaphors for "moving together in life."

Utilization. When one or the other partner *pulls away* or attempts to *take all the weight* the partnership will fall

114 CHALLENGE OF EXCELLENCE

short of the mark. This is an excellent activity to encourage *sharing, trust, and fully extending oneself.* There is a definite correlation between "feelings of being tall or stretched out" and actually being able to "walk tall through life." "Stretching out" extends us into endeavors in life that we never dreamed possible.

When a partnership is working well, we suggest that this pattern be used when an extra effort is needed to get what they want, in making decisions, or in assuming responsibility. We also suggest that they identify some outcome that will require a joint effort and imagine themselves being fully extended to achieve this outcome as they traverse the wires. In order for partnerships to work emotionally, they must work physically.

6. *The Kitten Crawl.* The Kitten Crawl requires *strength in both arms and legs, as well as flexibility.* It also requires a *stretch,* and openness in the pelvic region.

Utilization. The well–balanced person can support their own weight with both their arms and their legs. If the left upper side of the body is weak we understand that their thinking about their past makes them weak or they simply avoid thinking about their past. If the right upper side of the body is weak we understand that the person is lacking a vision or dream. We also understand that rigidity in the pelvic region signals that either their sexual energy is blocked or their basic life force . . . again the energy needed to fulfill dreams. Gentle exercise and softening of this region can result in a new freedom to dream, and access the energy to live the dream.

The Low Elements 115

7. *Swinging Tires.* Few people are able to complete this element. It requires *focus of attention, endurance, tenacity,* and *strategic thinking* to "keep a roll going." *Releasing* and "moving on" is also a requirement. Sheer *physical strength* is a nice plus.

Utilization. When a person needs to overcome several difficult obstacles in order to get what they want, we challenge them to complete the swinging tires. It is our hope that they can learn to accept a difficult challenge and complete it with strength, poise, and ease.

8. *The Fidget Ladder.* Complete awareness of the body and the ability to balance and move slowly are the primary patterns elicited by the fidget ladder. The person who falls short literally "flips out"! This element requires that both sides of the body be perfectly balanced and perfectly in rhythm. The bell at the top of the fidget ladder signals success.

Utilization. This is a funny activity and therefore one of our favorites. The slightest imbalance results in an immediate *flip out.* The look of surprise is both delightful and a gift to the player who hasn't been "*surprised*" in awhile.

116 CHALLENGE OF EXCELLENCE

This element can be adjusted for different outcomes. If it's a "surprise" that is needed, we tighten the ropes to increase the chance of "flipping."

Players often attempt to do this in a hands and knees position, buttocks in the air. What works is to extend fully and commit oneself to the task.

As in all elements, we use the well-balanced performance as an opportunity to connect this "excellence pattern" to real life. Key words mentioned about business, or personal life are mentioned as the participant climbs steadily toward the bell. The bell hopefully *re*-anchors the sound of the old familiar school bell so that the bell comes to mean "success" in the place of the failure or stress some knew in school.

In learning to bring into balance specific opposing concepts, it is useful to loosen the ropes to reduce the possibility of flipping.

The Low Elements 117

9. *The Flea Leap*. Very often growth and change means taking a sudden leap beyond what we perceive to be our every day abilities. The flea leap requires such a leap. The landing spot is small and precise. It is also of such a distance as to be surprisingly difficult. The first leap is down and out, the second up and out, the last down and out. Because the landing is so small, it is necessary to fully focus on and intend to be in "that spot." Unlike some of the low elements, this activity requires *courage*. The fall is higher than most and requires very careful spotting.

Utilization. This is an excellent activity to elicit patterns of *courage, intention, precision, balance,* and *trust*. On the first leap most players tend to *overshoot* the mark. The flea leap gives us the opportunity to fully support each other in a courageous endeavor. We challenge players to choose an outcome that requires both courage and a big change . . . a "leap" rather than a step. Sometimes we challenge a belief system when they leap, i.e., leaping from a belief that "receiving help is weak" to "receiving help is smart and efficient."

Players also experience strong feelings of being helped and helping on this element.

10. *The Hickory Jump.* The hickory jump is one of our favorites, and it prepares players for our favorite high element, the pamper pole. The major patterns it elicits are: (1) the ability to *go for it*; (2) the ability to *stretch and get what you want*; and (3) the ability to *hold on to what you get.* The perches allow for gradual risk in going for the trapeze. Once again, strong group support and spotting are required, as courage and trust are required.

Utilization. We have each player imagine, hear and/or experience something that they would love to be able to "go for"! That outcome is put on the trapeze (a visualization, sound, or feeling). The more difficult they believe it to be, the farther away they are challenged to stand. The farthest leap requires concentration, focus of attention, and a full extension. If a player is prone to "look away from their outcome" it will show up immediately as they appear to stop in mid–air. The player who doesn't trust

The Low Elements 119

that they can get their outcome will often close their eyes, rather than see the trapeze all the way into their hands. The person who "feels unworthy" of getting what they want will continually let go of the trapeze, rather than hanging on.

Getting what we want in life requires a risk . . . the risk of *going for ourselves* and *believing we can get what we want and being willing to go for it.* This element helps us *sort* what a person is willing to go for. Remember again, before a person can "go for it" in spirit, they must be able to "go for it" in their bodies. This pattern signals the brain about a way to repeat the pattern in multiple other ways.

11. *The Log Jam.* The log jam is great for eliciting patterns of *cooperating with ease and harmony* between partners or among small group members (2–3). Players must first develop a strategy for moving the logs, and then communicate in such a way as to get partners to cooperate. The wires move progressively farther apart so that developing an *easeful* way to progress is favorable.

Utilization. Again we have the opportunity to help partners work together in harmony. As always, when they are operating elegantly we suggest that they consider this pattern as a way of working together, living together, and/or loving each other. We sometimes attempt to approximate any handicaps that may exist in a relationship by blind–folding one or both partners or limiting the use of their limbs. Where handicaps actually exist, it is useful to help partners find a workable way to perform together.

120 CHALLENGE OF EXCELLENCE

13

CALIBRATING A GROUP

Both management and families are extremely interested in techniques for *team–building, motivating teams, decision–making, creativity,* and *developing leadership skills.* Most styles of training in these areas are hypothetical situations and are either boring due to familiarity or easily dismissed as "only role playing." We prefer to access the *actual* patterns a person has coded in their nervous systems. We, therefore, spontaneously challenge players to find ways to solve rather complex problems that actually requires risk. In these situations a person will offer us exactly the patterns they have available to them when caught "off guard". These are the patterns that we attend to most. All activities are video–taped so we can play them back and study patterns.

122 CHALLENGE OF EXCELLENCE

TYPICAL ROLE FUNCTIONS THAT
PLAYERS ASSUME

After observing a player's performance in a minimum of two group challenge activities we can pin–point these specific group role functions:

- The Chief who choreographs the outcome and maintains high morale and good group rapport.
- The Chief who takes undue risks.
- The Chief who loses the group and creates distrust.
- "Number two" players or good "right arm people" . . . the advisor to the chief.
- The Scout who goes first and paves the way.
- The clan hero who assumes the most daring position.
- The medicine person who helps each group member find their own power and place.
- The grandparents who make sure each player is safe.
- The warring warrior who is always accusing, disbelieving, or focusing on what is wrong and unfair.
- The peaceful warrior who resolves dissention.
- The renegades who pay little or no attention to the group process and remains disassociated.
- The heavy weights of the clan.
- The cheerleaders or songmakers of the clan.
- The clan clown, responsible for "lightening up" stressful situations.
- The sacrificial lamb of the clan.
- The clan thieves who will require group support but give none.
- Clan orators who love to hear themselves talk.

In addition to observing roles within the group, we are able to see specific patterns of behavior that players use in a group. Some are more useful than others. Our primary focus on group activities is on safety and getting the outcome within the allotted time. We notice what works and doesn't work. We also notice specifically *how* something works or doesn't work.

PHYSICAL POSITION IN THE GROUP THAT DEFINES A PLAYER'S ROLE — "TRACKING".

- The emergent *chief* will invariably move front and center in a group. This position demands attention simply by its placement.
- *Advisors to a Chief* will move in beside or somewhere close by the leader. These players may interact with several others but they are usually the last to interact with the chief before some action is initiated by the group.
- *Renegades* will literally move out of the group and completely disassociate or pace on the periphery of the group.

124 CHALLENGE OF EXCELLENCE

- The *Scout* will often remain on the periphery, check out what is happening and then move to the center. They are often the first to go out in front.
- The *Medicine Person* will move from player to player, often talking with, touching, encouraging, supporting others. Their concern is with each individual as well as the overall outcome.
- The *Grandparent* will keep a close eye on each person, making sure that each will be safe and nurtured by whatever plan is chose. they will disagree with any "sacrifice."
- The *Clan Hero* will often go last and perform the most difficult feat . . . often alone.
- The *Warring Warrior* mutters under their breath, complains, turns away from the group, speaks in staccato and/or loud voice tones which the group hears but doesn't respond to. They will appear "bossy". The outcome will be more important than fun and safe means.
- The *Peaceful Warrior* calms everyone down, encourages the weaker or afraid, is more responsive to the "warring type", etc.
- The clan "*Heavy Weights*" literally bear more weight than lighter clan members. Physical strength and agility is elicited and they rise to the occasion. They can naturally and easily carry a bigger load.
- The clan "*Cheerleaders*" or "Song Leaders" are spontaneous and use their voices to spur the others on. They speak louder and faster than others and the group moves at the sound of their voice.
- The clan "*Clown*" makes light of even the toughest situation, relaxing everyone and allowing for a clarity of thought. When they speak the group lightens up, breathes, and very shortly thereafter, acts.
- The *Sacrificial Lamb* of the clan. When the out-

come is unknown the sacrificial lamb volunteers their life for the clan in order that the clan may have information about how a plan will work. They often act spontaneously and the clan seems left in a stupor when they "bite the dust".
- The clan *Thieves* will be those who are more frightened or heavier than others and will require lots of literal "support" from the group. However, when others are performing they will disassociate and pay very little attention to what is going on. The "cost far more than they are worth".

There are many, many other roles which may emerge; these are simply those that are most often repeated in our experience. The important thing is to realize that the role a person assumes in a survival (high) game is the same role they will assume under the normal pressures of life. They must, in that they can only run the patterns that are coded on their nervous systems. IT IS USEFUL TO CHALLENGE PLAYERS TO TRY ON DIFFERENT ROLES IN ORDER TO ADD ADDITIONAL PROGRAMS OF FLEXIBILITY TO THEIR BEHAVIORS.

126 CHALLENGE OF EXCELLENCE

14

CHALLENGE ELEMENTS FOR GROUPS

We utilize the following four GROUP ELEMENTS to elicit information about how a person will operate in a group. These are particularly useful for corporate structures or families that wish to work together as a unit. The idea is to always notice what is working in a person's behavior, recognize it and grow it. When a pattern doesn't work or is inflexible, we challenge the person to try a different behavior. Most often the person automatically is challenged to try something new when we point out what they actually did. In survival activities the players are unaware of their behavior. The video feedback is often both delightful and shocking.

THE NITRO CROSSING

The scene is always set in a different way which is reflective of the group. We may suggest that the group is standing at the edge of a precipice that seems to go on for eternity. Their challenge is to get their whole group over the precipice along with the **can of nitro**, which, of course must not be spilled. Water is the imaginary "nitroglycerine" and the precipice the ground between two specified shores. Sometimes we suggest that the crossing is a raging river full of barracuda or hot peanut butter. Whatever the illusion, the challenge is to find a way to get the whole group over the gap along with the nitro. On this challenge we usually set no time limits in order to see how they respond to any challenge. As for all group activities it is important to figure out how the FIRST and LAST person will get across without group support. The last person is, of course, completely alone in their effort. To touch the ground is a personal "wipe–out"; to spill the nitro wipes out the entire group!

THE REBIRTH TREE

Here the illusion is of "hopefulness." Most of us suffered some trauma in the birthing process. The rebirth tree is alleged to be a "new technology" from the space being that allows us to experience a new life on the other side. We imagine what we as a group want on the other side . . . something that all can agree upon. Each person is also asked to "want or wish for themselves" something that they actually want in their lives. The task requires a team effort, and once again someone must go first and someone must go last. The wires are "nonexistent" and the "rebirthing" must be through the hole in the tire. It's quite obvious that a person who can't fit through the hole will have to seriously consider the difficulty that they have in life of getting what they want.

Very good spotting is required as players come through head first on the other side. They can be "cradled" and let down gently.

THE ELECTRIC FENCE

We love to create multiple illusions about this group task. The group is always inside the triangle of wire and must get everyone up and over without touching the wire or the trees. They must also avoid putting any part of their bodies under the wire. Sometimes we costume in battle clothes and convince them that they are on Nightmare Island with only one way to escape . . . over the powerfully volted electric fence. The guards are changing duty and they have only 15–20 minutes to get everyone out. Only a log is available to help them. Sometimes we convince them that they have been captured inside a space ship and are being "beamed up to outer space" to be used as research subjects, never to return. They must escape. Sometimes we costume as Hansel and Gretel and the group unfortunately finds themselves in the huge oven of the witch with the heat turned on and only 15–20 minutes to escape without cooking. Whatever the illusions, the TASK is real. The group must move quickly to get everyone up and over. Again what is to happen to the first and last person? Safety is considered to be the most important thing . . . ALL group members must be safe.

THE 16 FOOT WALL

This element presents the most powerful of group challenges. To get an entire group up and over a 16 foot wall presents a very real threat and requires precise spotting and the utmost of attention for safety. At no time is anyone allowed to attempt the wall without their full commitment. Neither is anyone allowed to have their head lower than their feet in either going over the wall or assisting others. Often a rope awaits them at the top to assist other team members over. The illusion is that absolute safety awaits on the other side. The wall is infinitely deep and wide. The only way over is up the middle. If, at any point, the strategies of the group appear to be unsafe, the challenge is called off and the group learns the lesson "NO CHALLENGE IS WORTH ENDANGERING ANYONE." No family goal or corporate goal or outcome is worth it if, in the process, a valuable team member is hurt. It is acceptable and wise to "re-establish" a new outcome when safety or good health is a risk. Obviously the first and last person over this element truly earns the title of "hero". A good basis of support is also needed.

132 CHALLENGE OF EXCELLENCE

15

PATTERNS OF BEHAVIOR ON GROUP CHALLENGES

Any pattern of behavior is useful in the proper context. It is therefore difficult to make judgments about movement patterns apart from the actual response of the behavior. Keep this in mind as we review those patterns that we often observe in the group activities. The important thing to remember is to PAY ATTENTION to both the behavior and the RESPONSE it gets. Remember also that whatever pattern a person runs in these "real" challenges are those that they have available to them in other types of group challenges. TWICE IS A PATTERN! If you see a movement pattern twice or more in short succession it is most probably a habit and will be repeated outside the gaming session.

Acting impulsively without group support. Sometimes a player will immediately act without checking with the group i.e. grabbing the rope on the Nitro Crossing and trying to swing across alone. If the move is successful (usually it is not) it can spur the group to action. If not, it can stop the group and have them think through a strategy. Both seem

134 CHALLENGE OF EXCELLENCE

to be positive results for the group as a whole. However, we believe it to be unnecessary for one or more to be sacrificed for the group in most situations. This type of person often turns into the "sacrificial lamb." If this pattern is repeated you can know that this person is willing to take enormous risks for the benefit of the group, or is so thoughtless of the group as to "expose their position" to the adversary.

Immediate action for what is needed. This is a pattern that management would benefit from recognizing. It is the player who either sees or hears what is needed and immediately begins to act on the need, i.e., "We need a line to take the Nitro across safely." The players take off their shoes and begin tying their shoe laces together to make the line. This is also the player who sees someone beginning either an unsafe maneuver or a task that needs support. They will immediately move into position and silently offer the support.

Gatherer of information. The pattern is to stand somewhat disassociated from the group and observe the group action and needs. They then move to the center to share what they see.

A disassociation pattern. This is the person who hangs out on the outskirts of the group and offers no support or input. If all is going well they may move into the group to take their turn. If the person moves or talks on the outside of the group they will add to the confusion by distracting other group members and slow down the group process.

Holding back sharing an idea. The person will make a slight movement toward the group to share an idea and then hesitate or step back. They appear to be "polite" in that they wait their turn. Most often, of course, their turn never comes. They may also be seen holding their throat or mouth. This is a sure sign that they are holding back saying something. When a person holds back sharing an idea they are unusually dissatisfied with the results.

Assuming leadership with the body. This is relatively easy to do. A person simply moves to the center and stands firm.

Assuming leadership with the voice tone. Voice tonality is extremely powerful. In most situations the firm, strong, lower voice tone will cut through the chatter and command attention. In a time of sluggishness when the group needs a "push," a loud, fast, higher voice tone moves the group to do something. In the first case, the lower voice tone assumes control by appearing "knowing and calm." In the second, the faster, higher voice tone creates the illusion of a sense of "urgency." Either can be sued effectively. The least effective voice tone is the tone of "being critical or judgmental." In this case either the group acts without full commitment or attention or they have a polarity response and ignore the critical tone.

Checks out ideas before sharing aloud. This is the person who is seen talking quietly with someone and receiving feedback before risking input with the group. This person would be effective in second management positions where a higher up needs to be satisfied. This person may also be effective in sales in that they get feedback before making a final decision. They may lack the courage to make the really tough and spontaneous decision.

Pattern of joint leadership. This is noticed when two persons equally share leadership from two different sides of the fence, i.e., there may be a leader on one side of the

136 CHALLENGE OF EXCELLENCE

wire or "river" and one on the other. They direct the action of the team on their side as well as confer with the leader on the other side. These people will make effective leaders who are open to the idea of other strong leaders and seek cooperation and the exchange of creative ideas.

The "democratic pattern". This is the pattern of seeking everyone's full support, and input before initiating action. This is the type who will hold lots of committee meetings and prolong action longer than is necessary. The longer a group of people prolong "movement" the more energy they burn and the more confused the issue becomes. It is important that everyone understand the final outcome. Achieving an outcome depends on each person only doing their part. It isn't necessary for them to understand everyone's part.

Involved and trusting. This is the pattern of remaining completely attentive and responsive to what is happening though not having any ideas or knowledge of how to proceed. Every organization needs these "apprentices" . . . people that are willing to listen and act on someone else's ideas in order that the ideas may be tested.

In a constant state of confusion. This pattern is seen when a person looks down, up, around, off in the distance, chats to self, talks while instructions are being given, etc. Their bodies move in a random and awkward pattern; they burn enormous personal energy, getting nowhere, and distract the rest of the group from getting their outcome.

Needing to know before acting. This is the person who always asks, "What's it going to be like to do this?" They require answers before trying to act. THE KNOWING COMES IN THE DOING. The person who needs to KNOW before acting will be the person who slows down every process

Patterns of Behavior on Group Challenges 137

because it is impossible to really know before taking the risk of "living the question." In the positive sense, this person would be excellent in handling the details of gathering enormous amounts of details where details are necessary. Too many of these people in any organization stops growth, however. Their bodies often resemble a question mark (?) from the side. They wonder a lot, but fear acting to really find the answer.

Demanding more than an equal amount of attention and support. This is the person who talks loud, cracks jokes about themselves, gathers an audience before acting, but hangs out on the outskirts distracting others while other group members are needing support. They may well be the "life of the party" at times, but the death of success over the long haul. They often "act stupid" when the pressure is on. Clowning a bit to RELIEVE pressure when it is needed would be a more useful behavior.

Pushing others aside. When a person is observed literally pushing others aside when emergency action is not warranted, hurt feelings and dissention is bound to occur. If a person pushes others around in a game they will tend to do it even more so under the stress of everyday life.

Filtering for excellence. This is the person who finds something positive to say about everyone and freely compliments them on their performance. This person is vital for growth in any organization. WE GET WHAT WE FOCUS ON. If we focus on what is RIGHT AND GROW IT, we prosper. If we focus on what is wrong, we also grow that.

Filtering for what is wrong. This is the ole' "hard nose coach type." They believe that if they embarrass or harass long enough they will get a change. The person who is heard pointing out what is wrong will tend to stress people

138 CHALLENGE OF EXCELLENCE

and over the long haul will hurt both the morale and the productivity of any organization.

Pulling energy back together. This pattern is seen when the group is completed with a task or has somehow gotten scattered. The player will physically gather people together or call them together. Sometimes they are seeking the group's support for the job they did. They are sometimes smart enough to know that fragmentation equals decay and their overall concern is that people feel "a part of" and "supported."

16

UTILIZATION OF GROUP INTERACTION PATTERNS

The first challenge is to be AWARE enough to observe repeated patterns within a group and the impact that they have on the group outcome. It is far easier to find a way to UTILIZE an existing pattern of behavior than to effect a change. If a person tends to stand back from the group and observe, and then move to the center to share their ideas, they are excellent candidates for "advisors to the chief" or "Scouts" in the organization. Rather than trying to get them to be group leaders and sales managers, it would be far more efficient to utilize their global views to gather information. Michael is a sales manager for a large computer company. However, he has demonstrated on numerous occasions that he is an excellent and observant "Scout" and "Advisor." His company would be money ahead if they were flexible and creative enough to create a position for a person to attend conferences, workshops, and training programs all over the country in as many "new age" topics as possible. Sharing the essence of these "new age" ideas with top management may well give managers leverage in meeting the demands of our rapidly changing

140 CHALLENGE OF EXCELLENCE

times.

The player who requires details before acting would make an excellent researcher for a top level manager. However, to have this person be the manager is to slow down growth and most often frustrate everyone who is under their direction. The person who "bullies or pushes people around" is usually an ineffective leader, but will make an excellent ally to "sic on an adversary." They can handle and distract impending adversaries while effective managers can proceed creatively. The person who draws attention to themselves by "clowning" may be sent into a situation where there is sustained stress and little humor. The presence of such a person will "break the pattern" and in so doing ease the stress. These are examples of UTILIZING A PATTERN. To do so requires FLEXIBILITY on the part of systems. Where flexibility is not possible, it is useful to attempt to alter behavior by ADDING ADDITIONAL CHOICES OF BEHAVIOR.

THE CHALLENGE TO ADD NEW CHOICES

In almost all cases we enjoy both UTILIZING and recognizing a pattern as well as challenging a person to "try it another way" . . . "just in case the need arises for a choice." The idea here is not to take away a choice of behaving, but rather to "ADD A CHOICE." By having a person "TRY IT DIFFERENTLY" we ensure that the pattern of choice is actually encoded in the nervous system and is available for the choosing.

The person who stands on the *sidelines* looking in is asked to see from the *center*. The person who goes *first* is challenged to go *last*. The person who holds back an opinion is asked to speak first, etc. Usually changes to the EXACT OPPOSITE will assist the person in having available all the choices in between.

17

THE HIGH ELEMENTS

After players have experienced the low elements and the group challenges, they are ready to proceed on to the high elements. Many "Challenge" programs believe that people should "fumble around on their own" until they either fail or find a way to succeed. Because we understand that the patterns that a person displays or creates are actually coded on their nervous system much like a program is punched into a computer, we INSIST THAT PLAYERS BE READY FOR AND SUCCESSFUL ON the high elements. Because the high elements appear to be the most risky, they are the ones that are best remembered. The more time, energy, and patience that we offer to the programming of success patterns on the low elements,the more success we know when we move on to the high challenge.

The experience of a day on the low elements and time working together solving group problems prepares the group to support each other in the air. Safety is insured not only by group support and spotting, but more specifi-

142 CHALLENGE OF EXCELLENCE

cally by a sophisticated system of seat harnesses, carabiners, ropes, wires, and pulleys of the highest quality and tensile strengths:

	Tensile Strength
ROPES—Kermantle, 10fall, 11 millimeter U.I.A. approved	5,000 lbs.
SEAT HARNESSES	5,500 lbs.
CARABINERS	5,500 lbs.
CABLES — Galvanized Aircraft	14,400 lbs.
PULLEYS	11,000 lbs.
SHEAR REDUCTION BLOCK (Pamper Pole)	15,000 lbs.
EYE BOLTS	22,000 lbs.
CABLE CLAMPS	12,300 lbs.
LOBSTER CLAWS	7,600 lbs.

The "Challenge of Excellence" ropes course consists of both **static** and **dynamic** belay systems. The word **belay** is a French term meaning **to be on safety line**. To be on **dynamic** belay is to be attached to an individual belayer on the ground who uses a figure–of–eight belay method to keep slack out of the rope and protect the participant from falls. To be on **static** belay is to be attached to the cable system above an element.

Before beginning the high challenges, all players are instructed on specific commands.

1. "On belay?" — called by the player to ask if they are securely attached to the safety system.
"Belay on!" — answer of the belayer to the player to assure safety systems are correct and secure.
2. "On climb?" — called by the player to ask the belayer if they are ready to have them climb.
"Climb on!" — answer of the belayer to let the climb-

The High Elements 143

er know that he or she is ready.

Other signals:

3. "Up rope!" — called by the player to ask the belayer to tighten the belay.

4. "Slack!" — called by the player to ask the belayer to loosen the belay. Slack is given at one foot intervals.

5. "Falling!!!" — called by the player the instant he or she falls.

HINTS FOR "COACHING" A PARTNER THROUGH THE HIGH ELEMENTS

1. Have everyone choose a partner. Partners should stay together throughout the course, one coaching while the other goes through an element.

2. Have partners work together to identify one to three outcomes that are very special. Each outcome should be coded with a "nickname", i.e., "Tiger Flower," "Zorro," "red," "eagle," etc. Also identify a sound for their state of excellence!

3. Pay special attention to your partner's use of the safety equipment; they may get excited and be less than attentive.

4. When coaching a person through the high elements, stay to your partner's right side. This insures that they will pay more attention to their bodies and less attention to internal dialogue.

5. Have your partner begin with a kinesthetic lead (weighted evenly on both feet or full–weighted on the right leg). This insures that the player will begin with full **awareness** of their bodies and their own "familiar voice" rather than some remembered voice of the past.

6. Remind them to begin each element in the Excellence Posture, i.e., heart out, eyes soft and focused on the

144 CHALLENGE OF EXCELLENCE

outcome, weighing on the heart spot (the balls of the feet), and breathing fully and continually.

7. Identify the outcome and give the code word for what they are going for. Use each element to "go for" something.

8. "Fire Off" their sound for excellence should they hesitate or get "stuck" in any way.

9. Pause at the completion of each element and REMIND them to breathe in fully the experience of succeeding.

Your and/or the partner's functions are several, then: To offer support and encouragement, to pay attention to their correct use of the safety equipment, and to help them utilize each element powerfully for themselves.

Coaching:

One thing which can make a great difference in the kind of patterns your partner programs for themselves is the ability to help them move gracefully through "stuck" places — where they feel afraid, frozen, or too tired to move on. Your confidence and firm coaching can help them learn to move right through the tough places. Calling for a smile, reminding them how they moved through another tough spot, challenging them, and being clear that they *are* setting patterns which they will want to be excellent ones are some ways to deal with these moments. By far the most powerful coaching at this time, however, is to break the task ahead down into the smallest, simplest chunks possible, and to give them a gentle command which instructs them. Anne had climbed the pamper pole, reached the top rung, and felt frozen, unable to turn herself around the pole and step up on the platform. Instructions were these: "Listen to my voice. I'll tell you exactly what to do . . . Feel your right foot on the rung where it is. Push yourself up with it until you feel yourself able to lie your stomach across

The High Elements 145

the platform. Rest there a moment, becoming aware of the support you feel. Now lift your left foot from where it rests on the rung . . ." etc. Start with exactly where they are and give them every move they need to get started again. As they "catch on" and start moving, you can cheer for them and let them do it on their own.

Hurray! They've succeeded and you have been a wonderful part of it.

The players are now ready to begin the ultimate challenges. Our challenge as leaders is to insure that the patterns they run on the high elements are used to bring patterns of excellence to the players' professional and personal lives. The patterns that are not useful are the same on the high challenge as on the low challenges. On the low elements we are concerned with noticing patterns

that don't work and offering choices. We insist on the high challenges that players perform with confidence, grace, poise, flexibility, and precision. It is here that we INSTALL PATTERNS OF EXCELLENCE THAT CAN ALWAYS BE USEFUL.

Each high challenge element is useful in INSTALLING A SPECIFIC pattern of excellence. Here we present each high element and the patterns that we find to be most useful to install.

Our particular High Challenge course is divided into three sections: The Pond–Side 7, The Pamper Pole, and The Secrets of the Magical Forest.

THE POND–SEVEN

1. *The Pole Climb.* We begin with a **dynamic belay.** "On belay?" "Belay on!" "On climb?" "Climb on!" The player begins a 20 foot ascension up the first pole. The pattern of **climbing up and supporting one's weight** in the process

The High Elements 147

is basic to growth. All patterns of **growth** require an upward movement. While the person is climbing we are suggesting such things as "You are climbing above your present situation." This brings this upward climbing pattern to any situations that the player feels currently "stuck in" or "unable to move."

2. *The Incline Log.* The incline pole ascends from 20 feet in the air to more than 30 feet in the air. A firm commitment and strength is required in each step. Because of the incline position the natural response is to crawl and lean forward to make the climb. However, one can discover that walking upright as one would walk down the street is actually the easier way. To "walk upright, balanced, with full intention" while ascending to a higher goal is the pattern we install here. We ask that the player put an outcome currently above them on the end of the walk. We challenge them to walk slowly, in control, balanced, and fully intending success upward toward this goal. Should they need the full or occasional support of the belay line, it is available. If they use the support, we ask them to consider specifically **who** it is in their real life that can be

148 CHALLENGE OF EXCELLENCE

that support. No matter how they negotiate the element, they are assured that they have a successful pattern for getting what they want, even if they have to **crawl** to get it. Again, UTILIZING the pattern installed for success is the ultimate outcome. It is important that people understand that their mere involvement brings them physical patterns of success necessary to "live their dreams."

3. *The Burma Bridge.* To most players, this element is similar to memories of actual or observed "war time" passageways across high and dangerous places. It also requires a firm hand hold and the ability to walk a straight line, placing one foot directly ahead of the other . . . moving directly toward an outcome. It is also shaky and requires that the person move from a "dynamic support" (held by a player) to a "static support" (dependence on one's own ability). As participants switch themselves from **dynamic** to **static** belay systems, we remind them of **changes** or **switches** they may want to make in their lives. All of these patterns provide the metaphor for installing patterns of excellence on the Burma Bridge.

The High Elements 149

If a player is to be confronting a battle (divorce, legal, competitive . . . as in sport, or verbal — as in business negotiations) we suggest that this walk is the passage way over the "dangerous waters." The player is challenged to place the outcome of battle on the pole at the end of the walk and go for it with soft intention. In a time of actual battle it is important that one have a pattern for moving DIRECTLY to the point. To dance in and out of battle is to expend a great deal of energy and assume undue risks.

150 CHALLENGE OF EXCELLENCE

4. *The Two Line Bridge*. Again support is dependent on the individual's own personal attention to "safety." With each change of the carabiner to a new belay point we remind the player to take personal responsibility for their safety... TO PAY ATTENTION... TO DOUBLE CHECK ALL SYSTEMS. It is our belief that the ability to nurture and "take care of ourselves" and each other has been dismissed as "the responsibility of someone else." As a consequence we have gotten ourselves into a situation of warring and hurting each other. The Two Line Bridge gives the feeling of limited support by sliding along the wires. It also very literally requires that a person walk "the line." In life it is often necessary that "we walk the line." In order to have the freedom and flexibility to play in our lives, it is necessary that we be able to enjoy and be successful at walking the line. This insures that we have the strategies to meet necessary time schedules and pull off

The High Elements 151

illusions of seriousness where it is "expected." As players negotiate the two line bridge we ask them to consider all the times that it might be useful to be able to "walk the line", e.g., to pull an all–nighter to study for an exam or prepare for a crucial client; to spend days pulling together tax information once a year; to prepare to teach when a regular has fallen ill.

Some folks believe that it's necessary to always maintain the stance of "walking the line." They will be extremely "inflexible" and often under stress since rarely do things go exactly as expected. Being "flexible" allows for our outcomes to be even better than what we first expected. Some other folks simply can not meet deadlines or fulfill expectations when the pressure is on. Being able to have a choice of "walking the line" is the choice of success.

5. *The Balance Beam.* If this element were on the ground, most would be able to walk it with relative ease. However, the fact that it is 30 feet in the air increases the illusion of danger and makes it an awesome challenge to walk gracefully. This is one of our favorite elements because it requires great balance and courage. Though one may choose to "hold on to the safety rope" it is more challenging to walk it with no hand support. If someone is "holding on" we challenge them to "let go" and in so doing "let go of whatever it is in their life that they have been "clinging to for support," even if they let go only for the last two steps. If they choose not to "let go," we ask them to honor who or whatever it is that offers them support for balance in their lives.

When negotiating this element we often have a player put a "worthy adversary" (someone or something that usually KNOCKS THEM OFF BALANCE) at the end of the walk. As they imagine this "adversary" we challenge them to walk fully balanced, with soft eyes and an open heart, breathing fully all the way to the end. The ability to do

152 CHALLENGE OF EXCELLENCE

this insures that the player can maintain balance in the face of any adversary.

Another technique for utilizing the balance pattern is to have the player imagine their dream at the end of the walk. Along the way we shout out the names of those things that we know throws them off balance and challenge them to maintain their balance no matter what comes. Both are extremely effective in bringing balance into their lives. A program of **balance** is a program of harmony with all things and moves us all closer to our dream of peace on earth and in our own daily experience.

The High Elements 153

6. *The Zip Line.* To ride the Zip Line is the final reward for taking the first series of high element challenges. The platform is first of all just that . . . a PLATFORM FROM WHICH TO LAUNCH DREAMS. It is **lofty** like all dreams, 55 feet in the air. It requires that one <u>TAKE A LEAP INTO THE UNKNOWN</u>! The player is belayed in from behind, requiring that they **trust** that they will be safe. The leap from the platform is considerably higher than 55 feet because it is also over a deep pond. The ride is over 100 yards or longer than a football field. The actual ride is like a "Peter Pan flight" and encodes a pattern of both flying and doing so **youthfully**.

When a player arrives on the platform they are asked to assume an "excellence posture" (heart out, eyes soft and scanning, and deep constant breathing). They are challenged to scan 360 degrees as they imagine having a "platform upon which to dream and express their dreams". In the process of scanning they are challenged to find a sound or word ("nickname") for their dream. To live our dreams is **always** a "Leap into the unknown" . . . and until the body actually has a neurological pattern for doing so, that is attached (collapsed or connected) to the key word for the dream, it is impossible to do little more than imagine the dream. To live a dream is to "take a leap of faith" that support will be there. For this reason, the ZIP WIRE is a very powerful challenge.

Having identified a sound or word for their dream the player is challenged to step up to the ledge and "jump into mid–air." They are challenged to do so with no "hesitation." To "hesitate on the platform" is to "hesitate in life" . . . and to hesitate in life is to miss the multiple opportunities that come our way to manifest our dreams. As the player jumps, we yell their code word in order to attach the actual neurological pattern of "leaping out" to their own way of remembering the dream. To remember their dream is to have their bodies feel the urge to "surge ahead"

154 CHALLENGE OF EXCELLENCE

and remember the "joy of the flight." The memory of "flying free" on the ZIP WIRE is powerful and gives the body information about what it means to fly and be free. Both of these sensations are realized as we risk doing what is ours to do in life.

THE PAMPER POLE

The second great challenge of the High Challenge Course is the Pamper Pole. It is so called because it is often so awesome a feat that one might wish to wear "Pampers®" on this one!

The pole climb is 34 feet to the top. The Climb is straight up and requires that a person be able to support their own weight when climbing to the top. The platform at the top is simply an 11 inch square . . . the size of a kitchen tile. The challenge of standing **balanced and exactly on the spot** with **nothing to cling to** is a respectable feat for anyone. When the wind blows, the challenge of balance is, of course, increased. From a standing position, a player has the opportunity to "GO FOR IT" . . . "It" being a suspended trapeze 8 feet, 4 inches away. In order to catch the trapeze the player must jump both UP and OUT. Few players actually catch the trapeze the first time or even after several tries. The challenge is mostly in the "going for it" and "extending oneself." CLIMBING, STANDING FIRM ON A SPOT, BALANCING, AND GOING FOR IT are the useful patterns in the PAMPER POLE. For the person who catches the trapeze, there is an additional

156 CHALLENGE OF EXCELLENCE

challenge to "hold on to what they've got." All of these patterns are powerful in assisting one to get what they want.

Again, it is useful to have the player put a lofty goal on the top of the pole as they make their climb. The ability to "stand, unassisted on the top" is the same pattern that we need to "hold firm to what we want" even when others would attempt to deny us the right to our position. It is useful here to have the player "identify that belief or position that they wish to have the strength to stand upon firmly."

Once standing, the challenge is to maintain balance without moving. This is perhaps the most elegant of opportunities to utilize THE EXCELLENCE POSTURE. There is no other posture that will allow the player to stay on the pole. We often attach key words for perceived problems to this posture by simply talking about the topics they may have mentioned as being problematic. Jim was afraid to speak his mind to his boss for fear of being demoted. We challenged him to actually say what was on his mind while standing on the pamper pole. There is no doubt that he was able to speak with precision (this is the only pattern possible and stay balanced) and do so with feeling of "standing up for himself." He was literally doing this as he spoke. We encouraged him to imagine a picture of his boss just in front of the trapeze and to see what he wanted as a **result** of his talk with his boss **on** the trapeze. This assures us that when he actually sees his boss he will automatically have available this "posture of excellence" as well as his OUTCOME beyond his boss.

It is our belief that the biggest problem can be approached differently if a person is able to remain "balanced" in the face of it. We therefore use the Pamper Pole to install patterns of excellence in the really tough places.

The High Elements 157

This is also true of really "tough" desires and dreams. Some aspirations promise to be particularly difficult, i.e. to risk being without financial security in order to explore and accomplish a personal professional endeavor. Likewise, we use the pattern of the Pamper Pole leap to have the person go for their outcome with courage and strong intention. "Going for our dreams" is the only way we can possibly ever realize our potential. When a person actually "catches" the trapeze they sense a "promise" that their efforts will be rewarded.

158 CHALLENGE OF EXCELLENCE

The High Elements 159

SECRETS OF THE MAGICAL FOREST

Some players insist on more challenges than others. We aim to please! The 4 challenges of the Magical Forest insure that each player has the opportunity to "stretch." Since the player who strives on Challenge is often the type of person who takes lots of risks, the elements in the Magical Forest intend to install patterns to "get through the tight places and the shaky places."

The Walinda Walk. Many of us remember the Carl Walinda family and their delight in walking tight ropes over lofty places and deep canyons. For those who remember seeing Walinda walk over the Grand Canyon or Taluela Gorge in Georgia, the Walinda Walk definitely equals "matters of life or death." The challenge is to walk a tight rope 30 feet in the air holding only a long balancing pole. Facing the threat of death or even social annihilation and overcoming the obstacle is to understand the "indestructibility" of the human spirit. The closer one moves to understanding their own "indestructibility" the closer they come to understanding "oneness" and "harmony" with all things. The Walinda Walk asks a person to face the worthy adversary of metaphoric death and walk through it. We often ask the player taking this challenge to consider what risk they desire to take that could mean the "end" of something. They are asked to put that level of challenge on the other end of the walk and go for it.

The Heebee Jeebee. The challenge of the "Heebee Jeebee" is in the middle of the wire. There is a point at which a player is squatted on a 30 foot tight wire with only the wire itself to hold on to. One is certain to *have the heebee jeebees* and to have "to get up off their buns when things are real shaky". In the fast world of business one needs this strategy in order to **recover** from those times that don't go as expected. The person who can't deal with "the heebee jeebees" or rise up from a **down position** simply can't handle the stress of taking the kinds of risks necessary to play and win the game of creative ventures. It is useful to have the player choosing this experience to consider the possibility of needing to "get up." For those people who live "sitting on their buns and shaking," this element provides the opportunity to teach the body how to GET UP AND GET ON WITH LIFE.

The High Elements 161

162 CHALLENGE OF EXCELLENCE

The Ropes Ladder. In order to descend from both the Heebee Jeebee and the Giant Swing it is necessary to climb a swinging rope ladder. This pattern is a true "Tarzan" experience and is useful to add fun and excitement to any climb or descent. The ladder swings free and simply requires that the climber stay erect and close to their support while moving to the ground.

The High Elements 163

The Giant Swing. Fans of Tarzan love this element. There is no way to literally swing from ring to ring without "*keeping a roll going*". To hesitate is to lose momentum and stop. The experience of swinging, hand–over–hand from one ring to another is the closest experience that most folks ever have of being Tarzan and "being Tarzan" is a powerful anchor for doing those tasks in life that bring abundance to both ourselves and our families. Each ring can represent a major reach in getting an outcome. The person who succeeds at the Giant Swing is considered a hero, which for many players is a powerful incentive to tackle personal challenges in life . . . nothing is out of reach!

The Dangle Duo. The final challenge of the Magical Forest is the Dangle Duo. Team work between partners is a necessity. There is no way for one person to accomplish this ask alone. There is a succession of intermittently spaced logs ranging from 3 1/2 to 6 feet apart. The challenge is to **climb together to the top supporting each other all the way.** Only the logs themselves may be touched (not the supporting wires on the side). This element gives immediate and specific feedback about how any two people will work together, whether they be marriage partners, friends, or professional colleagues. We almost guarantee that any two people that can elegantly accomplish this feat together can be assured of success in partnership.

18

CONCLUSION AND NEW BEGINNINGS

The information included in this book covers only two days of the seven day Challenge of Excellence Camp. These two days are used to discover people's patterns and to install new and powerful patterns of excellence. However, we only consider our work done when these new patterns have been tested repeatedly, and revised or extended if necessary. **THE CHALLENGE OF EXCELLENCE, VOLUME II; Playing The High Game** shares the rest of the story . . . or stories as it may be . . . The High Games: Indian Coup, Hunter–Hunted, Ambush, Finding the Light, the Medicine Wheel Walk, Chinese Wands and Feldenkrais lessons are a few of the highlights of opening and testing new patterns. Players' individual experiences in these activities provide the technology for the most innovative change work we know about.

The following story is an actual experience of one of our campers, and is reprinted with her permission.

166 CHALLENGE OF EXCELLENCE

REPRINT

Editor's Note: Based in Oak Park, Illinois, Rita Cashman is a business consultant, trainer and writer who teaches interpersonal communication and problem solving for managers. In pursuing her interest in the issue of personal power, and in a communications technology called NeuroLinguistic Programming (NLP™),[1] last November, Rita attended a week of excellence training with Dr. Scout Lee at the Broken Spoke Ranch near Stillwater, Oklahoma. Here's her survival report.

December, 1982

I met Scout Lee in the spring of '82, when she burst into a training session I was attending at the Radisson Hotel here in Chicago. For four days she had our group of 70 adults out running Indian games or scavenger hunts on Michigan Avenue — laughing, playing, and learning by quantum leaps. We learned about our own inner resources, our strategies for setting and achieving specific outcomes . . . and for exploring, risking, having fun, letting go . . .

Scout told us how she invited people to her ranch to go through a "high risk ropes course." People climbed a pole and jumped off the top. My stomach immediately said "No way, not me." Later Scout showed us slides of people playing and climbing and making that leap — and a little voice in me started to say, "Well, maybe . . . if those

---

1 NLP = NeuroLinguistic Programming: the study of how people take in and process information in a variety of contexts.

Conclusions and New Beginnings 167

folks can . . . I can."

So I borrowed a tent, down sleeping bag, some long underwear, and appeared at the ranch on November 14th (I knew that at the summer camps people took showers, etc. outdoors, so I had already verified by phone that in really cold weather, we'd have indoor facilities . . . I know my priorities.)

As you may know, I am a seasoned camper, having engaged in this remarkable form of entertainment at least two previous nights, back in my youth. I gamely picked a campsite reasonably close to the house and bathroom, and hurried to pitch my tent as night and the temperature fell . . . Then over a hearty supper, I met my co –adventurers, a mixed bag of business people, therapists, a teacher, one judge, and Tony, who was six months pregnant with her fourth child. (Tony's husband Michael co–trained with Scout, so Tony had decided it was time to experience this rowdy operation her husband is involved in.)

That night, around our first campfire, amid the stories, songs and belly–laughs, Scout, Michael, and other staff trainers asked us, "Why did you come? What do you want from this week?" Some of us wanted to learn NLP. Some of us were vague. Many of us, including me, said something like, "I want to play, dance, be spontaneous . . . I want to have more fun." Within our jolliness, I sensed we were tackling some hefty life tasks.

About sleeping in the tent that first night: my strategy was to crawl fast into the sleeping bag with all my clothes on — so I stayed quite warm, mercifully ignorant till the next day that the mercury had dipped below 20 degrees . . . However, I did notice I had to cover my face with a sweatshirt, or my eyeballs got cold.

Monday morning, we had an indoor session, sitting around on piles of pillows, fires blazing in the fireplaces. Using some NLP technology, people speedily learned some basic skills in preparation for the ropes course — about

168 CHALLENGE OF EXCELLENCE

which, oddly enough, I felt quite calm. Coincidentally, by Monday afternoon, I developed some mild flu symptoms, felt rotten, and missed some of the meetings and the practice session on the low balance beam. It was probably just fatigue, or something I ate.

Tuesday morning, stomach queasy but stabilized, I headed out with the group to the ropes. We warmed up with some "new games" activities, trust falls, tossing each person into the sky and catching them . . . We practiced negotiating over some low balance beams (logs, or two–by–fours or taut wires). A camera crew from *PM Magazine* was filming us that day — and the crew got tossed and caught like everyone else.

After lunch we paired up to tackle the high ropes. Wearing safety harnesses, you gradually climbed up and balanced along two–by–fours stretched precariously from tree branch to tree branch, then climbed a free hanging rope ladder, walked on a taut high wire with a parallel wire at arm's reach above our heads . . . They said the first "incline log" was the hardest.

My turn. Bill, my partner, was near me on the ground to help me through. I took my first steps onto the incline log — and I felt a rush of adrenalin through my body unlike anything I've ever felt before. Ever! "Terror" my inner voice named it. (Later I renamed it, but not yet.) I suddenly knew what my stomach had been churning about. My tennis shoes slipped on the slanted log, and my legs froze. Gallant Bill tried coaching (and coaxing me) in various ways. He soon noticed that I had a tendency to stop breathing, so he began to simply breathe with me, matching my rhythm, saying over and over, "Breathe, breathe, breathe . . ." When I did breathe, I could sometimes move. With fits and starts, periodic panic, recurring seizures of immobility, I somehow passed over the first stretches of beams. I cheated some — grabbing at the safety line to steady me. I was amazed at how little my body seemed to know about how to balance me, and how much I needed

Conclusions and New Beginnings 169

or wanted something to grab onto.

Eventually, I reached a small platform above the tree tops where I hooked onto the "zipline" — a roller coaster ride down one hill and up another — only without any track or cars . . . Just me, hooked onto this cable. "Remember what you came for" someone called. "Go for it," the voice reminded me. "Ready?" the zipline man asked. Me: "Ah, well, OK . . . Go." I stepped off the platform — seemed to lose the universe for one second — then realized I was zooming/shrieking/laughing through space (at considerable speed) and it was FUN.

Then came the *high point* of the ropes course: the pamper pole . . . It's like a telephone pole, 4 1/2 stories high, with spikes for climbing, and topped by an 11" square platform. You climb up, and somehow maneuver yourself onto the platform, and then STAND on it. The pole creaks and sways a little. You look out (if you choose to) over the treetops for miles and miles. Beautiful sight. Getting onto the platform, however, is a bitch. Can't describe it — you'll have to do it to find out. When you do, you'll notice that there is no subway strap to grab.

Once on the platform, having enjoyed the view, you exit by jumping for a trapeze which is located about 8 1/2 feet away. Like you, the trapeze is now also 47 feet off the ground. People down below waited in silence as I contemplated my jump. I crouched, began to swing in the rhythm I'd seen other jumpers use, then I stopped. "You're not serious" the voice in my stomach said. "Well, you can't stay here forever," some other voice replied. We negotiated for a bit. I crouched and started my swing again . . . "One, two, three . . ." My stomach voice imagined me still counting at "forty–seven, forty–eight." "No good," that other voice said: "You'll really have to just decide, and then just do it." "OK. On the count of three . . ." Crouch. Swing. "One, two, three, 3 1/8 — and <u>GO</u>." I jumped.

No, I didn't catch the trapeze. From the ground, they

170 CHALLENGE OF EXCELLENCE

said they saw my hand go *past* it — so I figure I was an inch or so low . . . Back on the ground, people caught me as I was lowered and freed from my harness — hugs, kisses, cheers — My body celebrated by shaking for another 30 minutes or so . . . and I still get quite a rush of adrenalin when I relive the moment. Only now, it feels kinda pleasant, more like "excitement," or "energy." Maybe next time I'll catch the trapeze.

The next day we re–enacted key moments from the ropes. Using NLP, the staff helped us identify our strategies for getting stuck, for moving, capturing the formulas for excellence so we could be sure to take them with us into other contexts. This is one feature of the week which sets is apart from many other outdoor/challenge type training experiences.

Wednesday night we played an Indian game out in the pasture. No moon, no stars, strange terrain, only a distant Indian whoop to guide us to our destination. I learned that my body could *feel* where to walk or crawl . . . much better than when I could see. I traversed the field with our tribal chief, Dennis, a brilliant, serious Chinese Canadian hypnotherapist, who was "protecting" me. It occurred to me, as we crept or crashed through the underbrush, Dennis in his brand new tennis shoes, and I in my dress leather gloves and Sax Fifth Avenue jacket, that I was probably the only person in the universe to have crawled on my hands and knees through an Oklahoma pasture, with a Jesuit educated Chinese Canadian hypnotherapist who hissed instructions to me like, "You wait here, whilst I go on ahead." "Whilst." I chuckled a lot.

Along with the laughter, the week was threaded through with inward time, sometimes sad. Scout's splendid horse, Oklahoma Sunshine Magic, got sick and hovered near death. Butch, the fluffy black kitten, tangled with the dogs, and a few days later was found dead. Scout gave him an Indian burial. With milder weather, I grew attached to

Conclusions and New Beginnings 171

that tent and sleeping bag. I moved my tent farther away from the lights and house sounds, so I could hear more of the wind and brush and animals. In the soft night sounds, my own moods swung through every range, and I felt questions in my heart that had no answer.

Friday morning we played another game, this time in town on the campus of OSU. Scout and I had had an intense conversation about questions without answers, about not knowing . . . and that must have given her the idea. Before the game, she said to me, "Girl," (Girl: that's how she talks. Oklahoma, and all.) "you just don't know how to NOT KNOW. It can be fun to just not know. If you could just be retarded . . ." And so she assigned me to play the game that day as a retarded person.

She gave me a retarded partner, Jill (who has a brilliant retarded act). Scout got a little leather pouch, Shay gave me some change to carry in it, and I pinned it to my chest. Scout's mom (who had adopted me by now) gave me a note that read, "My name is Rita. In case of emergency, please call my mother at 372–6550." I put the note in my pouch.

As the game started, Ray appeared. Ray is a neighbor of Scout's and a U.S. District Court judge. Scout had just met him and invited him to camp, so all week, Ray would saunter in for the ropes course, or for the key games. Since Ray had no partner, Scout gave the lucky man custody of Jill and me. With our list of tasks to do in hand, we three set off: Ray, tall, handsome and respectable (in his own hometown), dragging an idiot woman by each hand. We got a lot of very interesting reactions from people as we made our way across campus, in and out of buildings.

In the student union, some of the "enemy" team saw us and gave chase — so we scattered for a minute. Finding myself alone in the cafeteria near the kitchen doors, I efficiently decided to carry out a task: I would get someone to give me some food. I began to ask for cookies. "I

172 CHALLENGE OF EXCELLENCE

want cookies." I asked maids, kitchen workers, students, other university employees at the nearby tables. Some gaped, pretended not to see, got alarmed or scared; some tried to help, asked me questions, or gave me information, like "If you want to buy cookies, you have to go to the North Mall." I did not understand "north mall" so I simply kept asking for "coo–kies." Few people had any food left on their plates at this point — but I persisted, with my halting walk and dim eyes, innocently asking for cookies, with no success.

At last, a handsome young black man whom I had not seen before, walked up and handed me two wonderful sugar cookies in white waxed paper . . . I lit up, it was such a perfect gift — and so simple. I somehow thanked him with my face, took my cookies and happily walked out some nearby glass doors. Just outdoors, I sat in the middle of the sidewalk and started to eat my cookies.

Within three minutes, I was surrounded by the manager of the cafeteria and several other women employees, who asked me if I needed help, was I taking a class here, did I live at the sheltered workshop. I answered yes to everything, and finally produced my note from my mother. The manager read it, said "Oh, I see," and took me into her office to call my mother. As we walked through the huge kitchen, I gawked at the strange sights, and one of the women said tome, "This is our kitchen. It's BIG." "Big," I said. Only then did I feel the corners of my mouth twitching.

Well, they called my mother, and then kept me a few minutes until someone could come to pick me up. Not knowing how I'd really ever exit from this scene, the manager and I somehow made small talk. She asked me what I did at the sheltered workshop, and I described how I "put the little blue things . . . in the . . . bag, and I tie the bag . . ." Then Ray and Jill and Chris burst around the corner. "Rita, we told you not to wander off like that!"

Conclusions and New Beginnings 173

At first, the manager was not going to give me to them. "Wait, what is this? Her mother is coming for her!" Jill and I exchanged affectionate retarded greetings. Ray had his "I don't believe this is happening" look on his face. It was great.

Later at Murphy's bar we all shared our stories — there had been many adventures, pranks, kidnappings, and general mayhem . . . all good for lots of laughs. I proudly told how "they called my mother" and showed off my lovely gift cookies . . .

The next day, *PM Magazine* came back to shoot some footage out around the campfire. We were still celebrating on our hunter–hunted adventures, and sorting out the learning from them. They filmed as I reenacted being retarded. With luck, I could be on national television as a retarded person — just the kind of publicity any business consultant needs. I love it.

There were many other special moments. Dancing on Friday and Saturday nights. Some final games and schemes. A long barefoot walk on Saturday afternoon, through quiet woods and pasture. Time to lie wordlessly on the deck in the November sun. Finding Dennis on a sunny Sunday morning, up in a tree, singing.

I tell a lot of people about this adventure — especially about the Pamper Pole and being retarded. At least, I tell them what I **did** . . . but not so much about why, or what it all did for me. On that, I simply don't know what to say. Oh, I see that it all has to do with risk and never knowing before it happens; — With just doing it, and finding out . . . Scout calls it "living the question" . . . words I don't understand, but find them drifting through my thoughts as a gentle refrain . . . and blending back into the whisper of the night breezes near my tent, and then images of bare branches cradling a new sliver of moon. The Indians say the full moon is completion, the new moon is beginning.

174 CHALLENGE OF EXCELLENCE

All I know is that no two moons are alike . . . or camps, groups, ropes courses . . . you, or you, or me . . . Each of us each time, is different. When I go back, as I surely will, there will be new ways to play and laugh and cry. Whenever, and however, you take your next leap, yours will be totally unique and perfect for you.

* * *

This book has given you a taste of the **utilization** of movement. You have learned to notice patterns and find enormous amounts of useful information there. You have learned how to introduce new patterns to create programs of excellence in those with whom you live and work.

As you now recognize, you will be able to take this model and apply its concepts and principles in every aspect of your life. You have learned the **ropes of change** and can apply them whether on a high challenge course or in your everyday situations. If your wife has a pattern of always going last after everyone else is taken care of, give her the privilege of being first for awhile. Notice that one individual in your company is always trying new things and use them to "scout" new information for you. Notice how a man's voice tone and light–heartedness relax and calm your staff, and use him in tight situations. If your family life is not moving well, take a dance class together. Before stepping into a challenging negotiation, balance on the balls of your feet and move every direction lightly, setting the tone of "being on your toes" and having all the possibilities available. Meet your potential new business partner in a lovely park and walk forward together with ease in a beautiful setting. You may even want to do a trust fall off the conference room table with your new marketing team, creating cooperation, support and trust among them very quickly.

Pay attention to your daily patterns and habits, noticing what your movement in life is creating right now. Give yourself new choices for the fun and health of it. Challenge yourself to be your very best. Accept the CHALLENGE OF EXCELLENCE.

176 CHALLENGE OF EXCELLENCE

Metamorphous Press

Metamorphous Press is a publisher and distributor of books and other media providing resources for personal growth and positive changes. MPI publishes and distributes leading edge ideas that help people strengthen their unique talents and discover that we all create our own realities.

Many of our titles have centered around NeuroLinguistic Programming (NLP). NLP is an exciting, practical and powerful model of human behavior and communication that has been able to connect observable patterns of behavior and communication to the processes that underlie them.

Metamorphous Press provides selections in many subject areas such as communication, health and fitness, education, business and sales, therapy, selections for young persons, and other subjects of general and specific interest. Our products are available in fine bookstores around the world. Among our Distributors for North America are:

Baker & Taylor	The Distributors
Bookpeople	Inland Book Co.
New Leaf Distributors	Moving Books, Inc.
Pacific Pipeline	

For those of you overseas, we are distributed by:

Airlift (UK, Western Europe)
Bewitched Books (Victoria, Australia)

New selections are added regularly and the availability and prices change, so ask for a current catalog or to be put on our mailing list. If you have difficulty finding our products in your favorite store or if you prefer to order by mail, we will be happy to make our books and other products available to you directly. *Your involvement with what we do and your interest is always welcome* - please write to us at:

Metamorphous Press
3249 N.W. 29th Ave.
P.O. Box 10616
Portland, Oregon 97210-0616
(503) 228-4972

SKILL BUILDER SERIES

The Excellence Principle
Utilizing NeuroLinguistic Programming
Scout Lee, Ed.D.

Basic Techniques, Book I
Linnaea Marvell-Mell

Basic Techniques, Book II
Clifford Wright

Your Balancing Act
Discovering New Life Through
Five Dimensions of Wellness
Carolyn J. Taylor, M.N.C.S.

Advanced Techniques
Book I
Phill Boas with Jane Brooks

The Challenge of Excellence
Learning the Ropes of Change
Scout Lee, Ed.D.
Jan Summers, Ed.D.

NLP Series
from Metamorphous Press

SKILL BUILDER SERIES

The Excellence Principle

Scout Lee, Ed.D.
This standard in the field of NLP was originally a set of personal notes and formal thoughts. In its revised form, this workbook is packed with dynamic metaphors, ideas, exercises and visual aids.
1-55552-003-0 .... paperback $16.95

Your Balancing Act

Carolyn Taylor
This NLP text presents systematic exercises and new material for changing the all important beliefs that underlie the conditions of wellness. Health, relationships, creativity and success are just a few aspects addressed.
0-943920-75-2 .... paperback $12.95

Basic Techniques, Book I

Linnaea Marvell-Mell
This is the only NLP workbook available for those who wish to refine their NLP skills, people who have read books on the subject or attended seminars but want more. The book comes with a cassette tape. It complements the introductory book, *Magic of NLP Demystified* and reinforces NLP skills.
1-55552-016-2 .... paperback $12.95

Advanced Techniques

Phill Boas with Jane Brooks
This manual is designed for use by those who have some knowledge of NLP. It is written from the perspective of the trainer/ seminar leader, and much of the information is intended to help the group leader assist the participants to get maximum benefit from the 50 exercises.
0-943920-08-6 .... paperback $9.95

Basic Techniques, Book II

Clifford Wright
This workbook provides additional tools to refine skills learned in *Basic Techniques, Book I.* Filled with exercises for individual practice or group work, *Basic Techniques II* provides ongoing skill-building in NLP technology
1-55552-005-7 .... paperback $10.95

The Challenge of Excellence

Scout Lee, Ed.D., Jan Summers, Ed.D.
Scout Lee's book is about utilizing challenge and playfulness to program the human computer for excellence. It has sophisticated information on body language and its connection to the mental process.
1-55552-004-9 .... paperback $16.95

POSITIVE CHANGE GUIDES

Get The Results You Want
Kim Kostere & Linda Malatesta
This title provides an explicit model of communication and change which combines the state of the art behavioral technology of Bandler & Grinder with the optimism of humanistic psychology.
1-55552-015-4 .... paperback $13.95

Fitness Without Stress
Robert M. Rickover
This book explains the Alexander Technique, recognized today to be one of the most sophisticated and powerful methods of personal transformation available. This method can be enjoyed by readers with no previous experience.
0-943920-32-9 .... cloth $14.95

Magic of NLP Demystified
Byron Lewis & Frank Pucelik
This introductory NLP book is intended to give its readers a clear and understandable overview of the subject. It covers the essential elements of NLP and uses illustrations to further explain this behavioral science.
1-55552-017-0 .... paperback $9.95
0-943920-09-4 .... cloth $16.95

The Power of Balance
Brian W. Fahey, Ph.D.
The importance of balance in life is the emphasis of Fahey's book. It expands on the original ideas about balancing body structure, known as "Rolfing." Reading this thought-provoking text can be a step toward achieving high levels of energy and well-being.
0-943920-52-3 .... cloth $19.95

These are only a few of the titles we offer. If you cannot find our books at your local bookstore, you can order directly from us. Call or write for our free catalog:

Metamorphous Press
P.O. Box 10616
Portland, Oregon 97210
(503) 228-4972
OR
Toll Free   1-800-937-7771

Shipping and handling charges are $2.75 for each book and $.75 for each additional title. We ship UPS unless otherwise requested. Foreign orders please include $1 for each additional book - all orders must be prepaid in U.S. dollars. Please write or call directly to determine additional charges. Prices and availability may change without notice.